HOW TO READ HANDS

Other Works by Papus:

Exegesis of the Soul: Three Works on the Nature, Origin, and Destiny of the Human Soul

What a Master Mason Ought to Know

What is Occultism? Its Secrets and Reasons

Related Titles from Triad Press:

The Arcane Schools by John Yarker

The Baylot Manuscript in Translation

Grand Marvelous Secrets by Abbe Julio

The Little Religions of Paris by Jules Bois

Apostolic Church of the Pleroma Clergy Handbook by Tau Phosphoros

The Pleromic Light Unveiled by Tau Phosphoros

HOW TO READ HANDS
First Elements of Chiromancy

by
PAPUS
(Dr. Gérard Encausse)

Translated from the French by

Sâr Phosphoros

Sovereign Grand Commander
Christian Knights of Saint-Martin

Fox Lake, IL

How to Read Hands: First Elements of Chiromancy
by Papus

Translated by Sâr Phosphoros

Copyright ©2017, 2023 Sar Phosphoros.
All rights reserved.

ISBN: 978-0-9973101-4-6

Triad Press, LLC
123 S. U.S. 12
#33
Fox Lake, IL 60020

PREFACE	**IX**
FOREWORD TO THE FIRST EDITION	**XI**

FIRST PART: SYNTHETIC CHIROMANCY

CHAPTER I: THE LINES OF THE HAND — **1**
1. SATURN AND THE LINE OF FATALITY — 5
2. MERCURY AND THE LINE OF INTUITION — 5
3. APOLLO AND THE LINE OF THE IDEAS — 8
4. JUPITER AND THE HEART LINE — 8
5. THE THUMB AND THE LIFE LINE — 8
6. MARS AND THE HEAD LINE — 12
7. THE MOON AND ITS LINES — 12

CHAPTER II: READING THE SIGNS — **17**
1. ON THE EVENTS — 18
2. ON LUCK — 22
3. ON PHYSICAL LIFE AND ILLNESSES — 22
4. ON THE EGO — 25
5. ON SENSUAL LOVE — 26
6. MARRIAGE OF LOVE — 26
7. ON THE WILL — 26
8. ON AUDACITY AND SUCCESS — 29
9. ON THE SENTIMENTAL LIFE — 29
10. ON ART - ON FORTUNE — 32
11. ON SCIENCE — 32
12. ON COMMERCE — 34
13. TASTE FOR GLORY OR MONEY — 34

SECOND PART: ANALYTICAL CHIROMANCY

SOME WORDS ON THE HISTORY OF CHIROMANCY — 38

CHAPTER III: DIVISIONS TO ESTABLISH IN THE STUDY OF THE HAND — **40**

CHAPTER IV: ON THE STUDY OF THE SHAPES, OR CHIROGNOMY — **42**
1. ON THE HAND IN GENERAL — 43
2. ON THE HANDS — 46
3. ON THE WRIST — 47

4.	ON THE PALM	47
5.	ON THE MOUNDS	48
6.	ON THE FINGERS	50
8.	THE MANNER TO STUDY WELL THE SHAPE OF THE FINGERS	58

CHAPTER V: ON THE STUDY OF THE LINES OF CHIROMANCY — 59

1.	CAUSE OF THE OBSCURITY OF MANY CLASSICAL TREATISES: THE TWO CHIROMANCIES	59
2.	CHIROMANCY OF THE WRIST	65
3.	CHIROMANCY OF THE PALM OF THE HAND	67
4.	CHIROMANCY OF THE FINGERS	78
5.	CHIROMANCY OF THE NAILS	80
6.	THE MODIFYING SIGNS	81

CHAPTER VI: ASTROLOGICAL CHIROMANCY — 87

1.	ASTROLOGICAL CORRESPONDENCES	87
2.	INTERPRETATION OF THE SIGNS	91
3.	HOW TO DETERMINE, EVEN APPROXIMATELY, THE DURATION OF LIFE	98 98
4.	HOW THE HAND IS TO BE READ	100

THIRD PART: CHIROSOPHY

CHAPTER VII: CHIROSOPHY OR THE STUDY OF CAUSES — 103

1.	THE CHIROSOPHY OF THE SHAPES AND THE ASTRAL BODY	103
2.	CHIROSOPHY OF THE LINES AND SIGNS	108
3.	CHIROSOPHY OF THE HAND IN GENERAL	111
4.	COMPARATIVE CHIROMANCY	117

CHAPTER VIII: LITTLE DICTIONARY OF CHIROMANCY — 119

BIBLIOGRAPHY — 122

APPENDIX I — 127

1.	SOCIAL CONDUCT OR THE LETTER M	127

2.	THE STRUGGLE AGAINST FATALITY OR THE LETTER T	127
3.	DISCRETION OR THE LETTER O OR A	129
4.	ORDER IN THE ROOM OR THE LETTER I	129
5.	HOW ONE DRESSES OR THE LETTER D	129
6.	FINAL CONSIDERATIONS ON GRAPHOLOGY	130

APPENDIX II — **132**

APPENDIX III — **135**
   A. Graphology ("PHANEG") — 135
   B. Chiromancy (Mme. "FRAYA") — 138
   C. Physiognomy ("PHANEG") — 140

ENDNOTES — **142**

Preface

The little "Synthetic Treatise on Chiromancy" that we have extracted from our work on the Occult Science is rapidly exhausted, though printed in a great number of copies. We have benefitted from this new edition, become necessary, in order to give a greater importance to this work, all while preserving the simplicity and the general character to which it owes its success.

Thus we have preserved, while bringing to it slight modifications, our *synthetic study* which allows one in a few hours to learn the first elements of chiromancy. But we have believed it necessary to add a personal work on chirognomy and chiromancy, and some considerations on chirosophy, to allow our readers to approach the details, if the success that they will obtain with the first lessons gives them confidence, of which we cannot doubt. This new work forms, then, a complete whole; ending, moreover, with some bibliographical notes which will allow the seekers to delve even deeper into their studies. We have no doubt of the existence of possible defects in our work; but you will see that we have made the greatest efforts to remain original, and to avoid the obscurity inherent in the most celebrated works concerning this art.

Papus.

Foreword to the First Edition

It is curious to note that our era, when experimentation enjoys such favor, presents at the same time numerous examples of unconceivable bias.

Thus, with what sneers do the "serious men" receive all these ideas (of another age) relative to the impression of the mental upon the physical, and to the possibility of destroying the general character of an individual in the form of his organs! - There was, for the independent physician, a beautiful work to do with verifying, in the amphitheaters of the hospitals, on one or two hundred subjects, the truth of the assertions of the chiromancers as regards the possible indication of the length of life given by a line of the hand. - So long as experiments of this kind will not have been made, how can one pretend to set himself up as the "school master" of this subject?

The books treating on chiromancy all present a capital defect, in our opinion. The spirit of the reader is entangled in that minutia of little details with which these works are replete. Our aim, in making this extract from the *Traité méthodique de Science Occulte*, is to provide the reader with some very general, and at the same time very precise, ideas on the question, in order to put him in a position to classify later on the details that he will find in the ordinary treatises on chiromancy.

We think, counter to all the opinions made, that the experimenter has the right to approach all the fields of action furnished to his activity, and that the various ideas concerning divination may interest him as much as the study of archaeology or linguistics.

For our readers to become our collaborators, and soon our master in this curious research - that is our most ardent desire.

Papus.

FIRST PART
SYNTHETIC CHIROMANCY

CHAPTER I
The Lines of the Hand

Our study would be incomplete if we did not at least give the fundamentals of the sciences called: "divination."[1]

I am well aware that those ignorant of the Occult Science claim that these sciences of divination are entirely false and cannot give any serious result. The facts come each day to do justice to these beautiful words.

One process, beloved of the contemporary critic, consists in judging a work only on the points concerning these kinds of studies. It is thus that, for Larousse[2], my work on the Tarot is reduced solely to the chapter dedicated to the ladies and devoted to cartomancy.

Be that as it may, as my care is, above all, to be complete, I am going to develop the principal ideas of one of the oldest sciences of divination known: Chiromancy (reading the hand).

Applying the Occult Science to the theory of Chiromancy, I am going to present this art in a completely new light, giving teachings that one would seek in vain in the modern treatises on the question. These treatises, especially that of Desbarolles, will be useful to consult for detailed analyses. I will content myself in this chapter to consider the question under the purely synthetic point of view.

It seems useless to me to respond to the objection that the lines of the hand are the result of the special occupations of the individual or of the natural folds of the skin. Only a medical doctor may indulge in these errors of observation.

The left hand, which works less, has many more lines that the right hand; and the newborn infants, who have not yet chosen, that I know of, any particular profession, have a great number of lines. As to the natural folds of the skin, the observations made according to the ideas of chiromancy will show their true role better than all the possible and impossible treatises on anatomy.

Let us consider the hand (we generally take the left hand as an example) in a synthetic fashion; what do we see here?

A series of organs which are nearly incapable of moving separately: the four fingers; an organ which is opposed to them: the Thumb.

The ensemble of fingers will represent the ensemble of impulses given to the individual. The Thumb represents, on the contrary, the possible action of the individual on these suggestions; the acceptance or refusal of the impulses given.

Each finger represents one suggestion particularly. We will soon have to look at these divisions in detail.

Take note of the various heights occupied by the fingers. What do you see?

The tallest of all, the one which rules the assembly, is the *medius*, the middle finger.

On each side of this finger you find two others, a large and a small one on each side. On the right: the *Ring-finger* and the *Little finger*; on the left: the *Index* and the *Thumb*.

You may therefore compare this medius to a balance whose scales are formed by the fingers situated on each side.

We will therefore rediscover here our universal ternary, the two opposed (the two scales) and the support which unites both (the medius).

In the middle, which rules all, is the unavoidable Destiny, Fatality, the somber Κρονος - SATURN (astrological name of the medius).

To the right of Fatality: Dream, Theory, and Ideal, represented by the two fingers:

APOLLO (the ring finger) - Art.

MERCURY (the little finger) - Science.

To the left of Fatality: Reason, Practice, the Positive represented by the two fingers:

JUPITER (the index) - Honors.

VENUS (the thumb) - Will - MAN - Love.

Let us summarize the names attributed to each finger:

- The MEDIUS: *Saturn*.
- The RING FINGER: *Apollo*.
- The LITTLE FINGER: *Mercury*.
- The INDEX: *Jupiter*.
- The THUMB: *Man and Venus*.

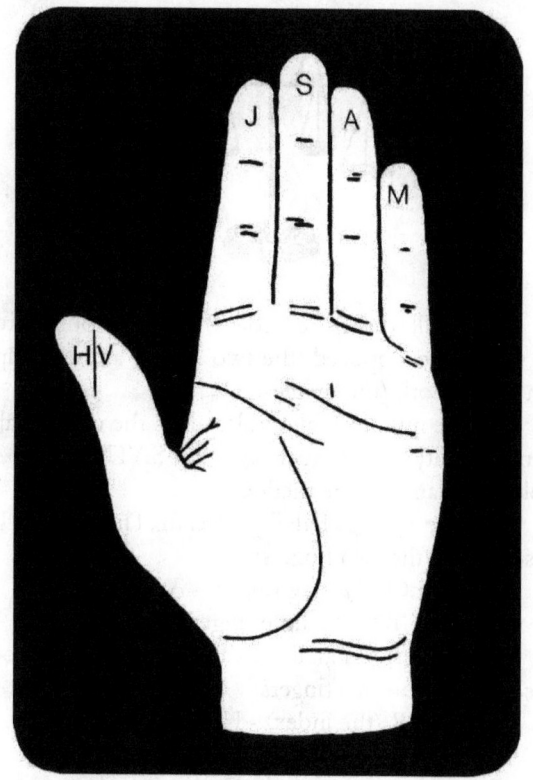

Figure 1
The astrological names of the fingers.
H-V: Man - Will
J: Jupiter
S: Saturn
A: Apollo
M: Mercury

Each finger includes:

1. *A projection* upon which it takes root. This projection has received the name of Mound. Each mound takes the name of the corresponding finger (Mound of Jupiter, Mound of Saturn, etc.);

2. A line which departs from this finger to proceed into the hand. This line is very evident or else absent according as the *suggestion* given by the finger is strong or does not exist with the individual.

Let us look at the course followed by each of the lines attached to a finger and the name of these lines.

1. SATURN AND THE LINE OF FATALITY
(Figure 2)

From the finger of Saturn departs a line which crosses vertically the whole hand to end near the wrist. *This is the line of fatality*; it will indicate events.

2. MERCURY AND THE LINE OF INTUITION
(Figure 3)

Mercury represents the practical side of the ideal; it is *Science* in comparison to art. It is also *Commerce* in comparison to invention.

Mercury was the messenger of the gods; the "reporter" of Olympus.

In the hand, the *line of Mercury* will be the line of the *intuitives*, of the *mediums*, of persons *nervous to excess*, subject to prophetic dreams (the little finger tells the nurses the children's secrets).

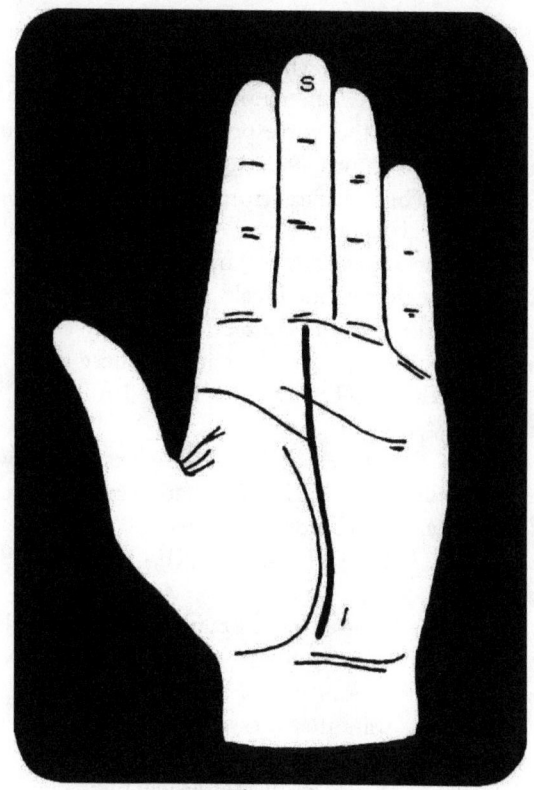

Figure 2
The line of fatality (*Saturnian*)

The Lines of the Hand

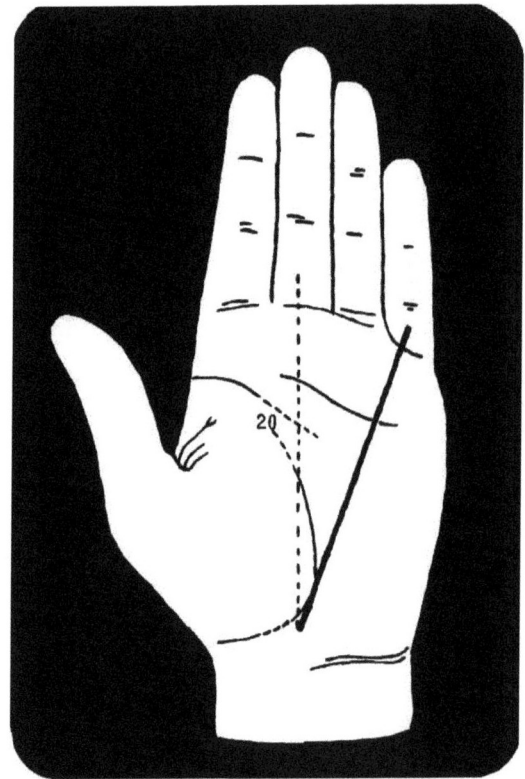

Figure 3
The line of intuition (*Mercurian*)

This line departs from the little finger and directs itself towards the wrist to originate nearly on par with the line of Saturn.

To keep oneself from the error which consists in believing that this line represents the *diseases of the liver*, it is the line of intuition; it is often missing.

3. APOLLO AND THE LINE OF THE IDEAL (Figure 4)

Apollo is the ideal in all its purity. It is art, it is invention, it is also fortune nobly acquired.

In the hand, the *line of Apollo* will be the line of the artists and inventors. It departs from the ring-finger and directs itself towards the bottom while often going towards the level of the meeting of the thumb and the wrist.

It is rarely complete. Very often it is divided into several fragments.

4. JUPITER AND THE HEART LINE (Figure 5)

Jupiter is the honors, it is the *ideal of the practical life*, it is also self-sacrifice, magnanimity, *the Heart*.

The *Heart line* departs from Jupiter or from its mound and directs itself *horizontally* (and no longer vertically) towards the little finger, at the base of the mound at which it ends.

It is the line of passion, of devotion, of anger. It is the line of ambition.

5. THE THUMB AND THE LIFE LINE (Figure 6)

The thumb is man himself in his three specifications:

- Above, the reason (1st phalanx).

- In the middle, the sentiment (2nd phalanx).

- Below, the senses (root).

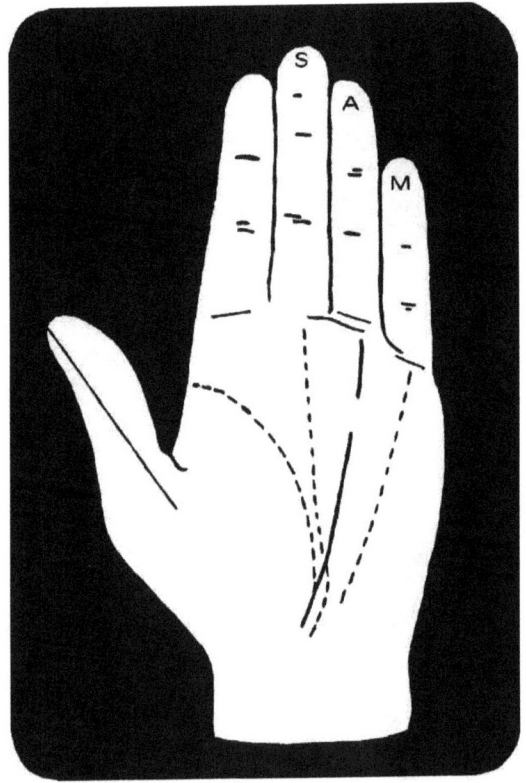

Figure 4
The line of the ideal (*Apollonian*).

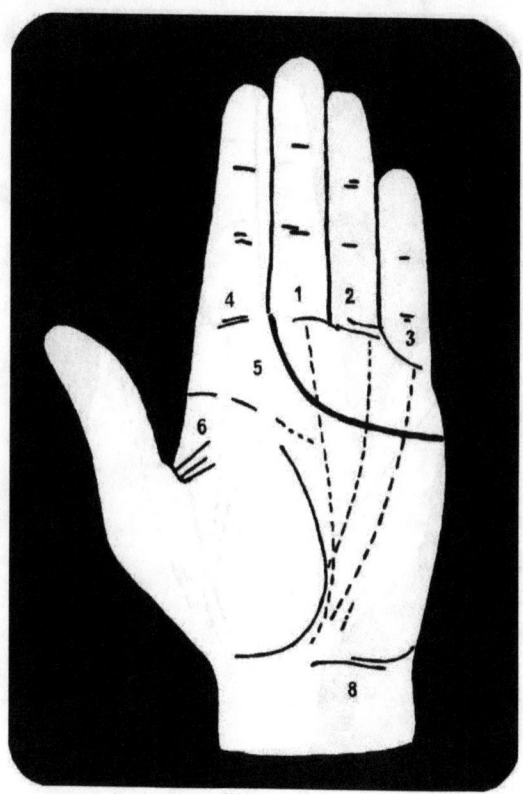

Figure 5
The heart line (*Jupiterian*).

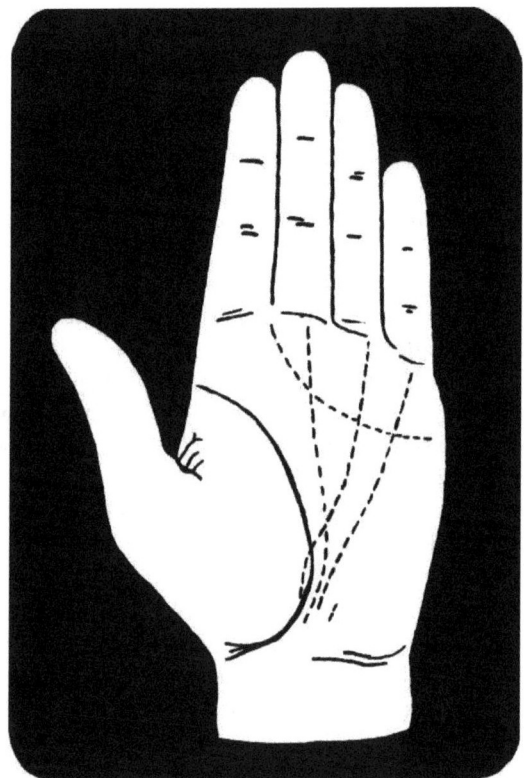

Figure 6
The life line (*Hominal*).

Man is surrounded by the *physical life* which marks the stages of his body.

Thus, the line which surrounds the thumb is the *life line*.

It is upon it that we will see, not the events (which

would be an error), but *the illnesses*, that is to say all that concerns the physical; the most material and practical side of man.

Other centers

Beyond the fingers, two centers ought to be considered:

1. The central part of the hand, corresponding to Mars.

2. The right part of the hand; that which extends from the little finger to the wrist. This part presents a bulge characteristic, attributed to the Moon.

6. MARS AND THE HEAD LINE (Figure 7)

Taking up the middle between all the other lines, we see one placed between the heart line and the life line and directed horizontally.

This is the *head line*, the line of action which streaks through the entire domain of the god of Activity par excellence: Mars.

7. THE MOON AND ITS LINES (Figure 7a)

The Moon presides over the imagination, and over all that pushes forth, over generation.

It does not have a line properly speaking; but it possesses a great number of them arranged in gradation on the entirely outer side of the hand.

In order to see these lines, the hand must be placed in profile.

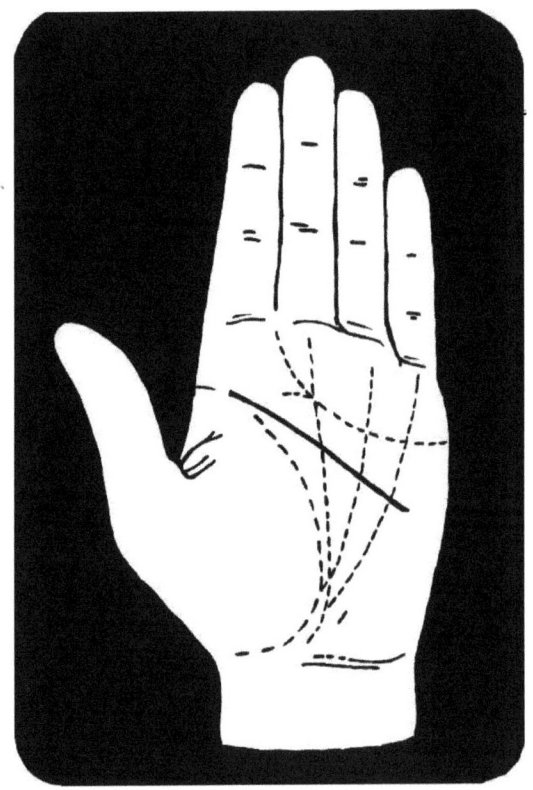

Figure 7
The head line (*Martial*)

How to Read Hands

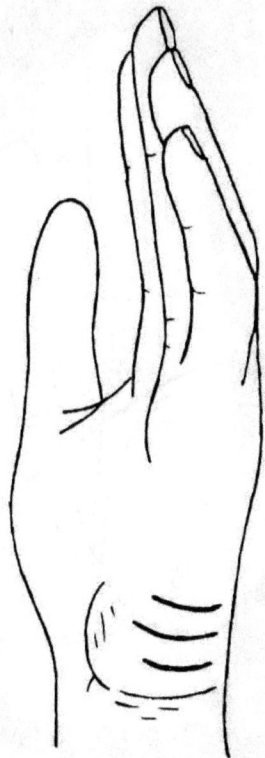

Figure 7a
The lines of imagination and generation (*Lunar lines*)

We have just laid out the construction of the hand and its different lines. Let us summarize what we have said in a composite figure.
(See Fig. 8.)
 1. *The Saturnian* (fatality).

Departing from the medius. In the middle.

2. *The Apollonian* (ideal).

Departing from the ring-finger. To the right.

3. *The Mercurian* (intuition).

Departing from the little finger. Extreme right (very often missing).

- Three horizontal lines:

4. *The heart line* (generosity).

Departing from the index. Left.

5. *The head line* (will, activity).

In the middle of the hand (horizontally).

6. *The life line*.

Departing from the thumb and surrounding it. Extreme left.

At the base of the wrist, a series of horizontal lines: the *Rascette*.

Furnished with these particulars, we understand the general constitution of the hand.

Let us look at how one may read therein the tendencies of the individual.

How to Read Hands

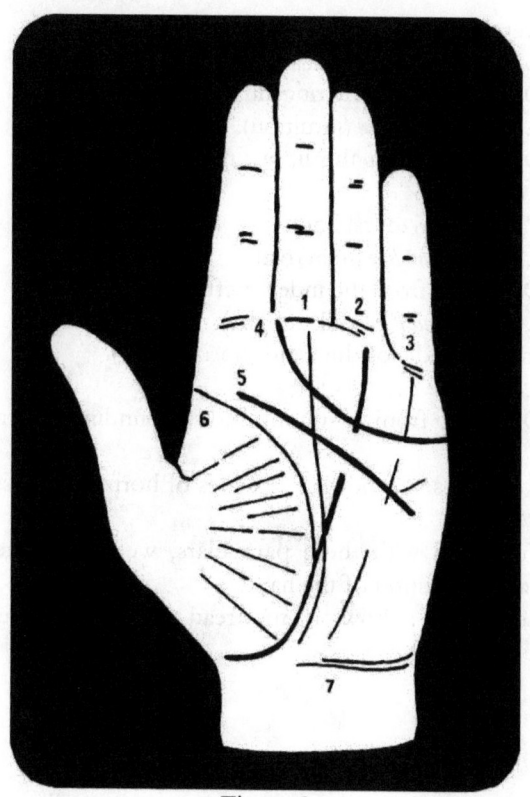

Figure 8
Composite

CHAPTER II
Reading the Signs

Two great principles struggle in man: *Fatality* and the *Will*.

Providence, the third of these universal principles, intervenes only accidentally and in a manner which cannot be foreseen surely.

The line of Saturn representing fatality, the head line representing the will, their reciprocal action gives us the first division that we are to consider. This action produces a cross indicated by figure 9.

To the right of this cross, will be the *ideal, theoretical* side.

To the left, the *practical* side.

All these lines which will go from the middle towards the right will indicate the *ideal* and *intellectual* tendencies of the individual.

All the lines which will go from the middle towards the left will indicate on the contrary, the *practical, material* tendencies of this individual.

Do you want to see whether someone is more ideal than material?

Look at the distance which exists between the head line and the root of the fingers, and see whether it is superior to the distance of this line to the base of the wrist.

Now let us see how to read the different presages.

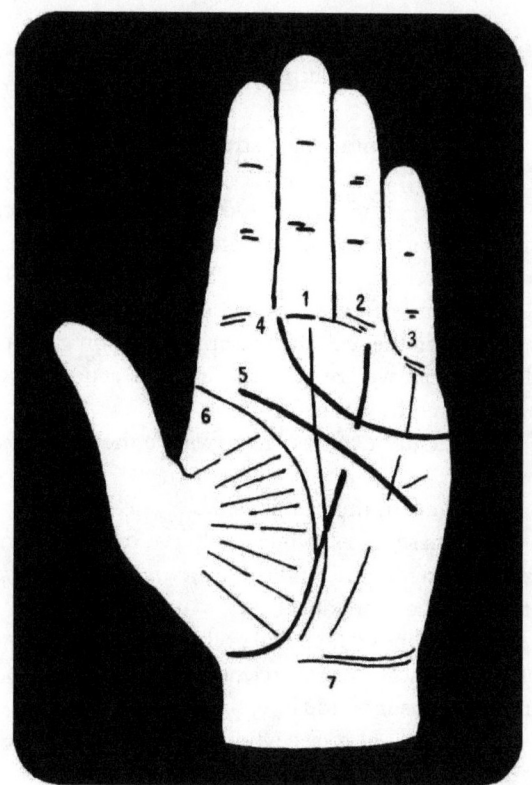

Figure 9
Fatality (*Saturnian*)
The Will (*Head line*)

1. ON THE EVENTS

The line of Saturnian Fatality indicates the exact era of events past, present, and future.

All which will somewhat modify the existence is

indicated by a leap of the line, by a break, or by another line coming to place itself across it.

The direction of this leap to the right or left indicates whether the event has influence over intellectual occupations or position.

A line of Fatality straight and without breaks is a uniform life from the point of view of events and ideas.

Here is how we see the ages (this is very important).

Follow on Figure 10.

The line of Fatality is cut:

1. At the very base by the line of Mercury or that of Apollo.

2. Higher by the *head line*.

3. Higher by the *heart line*.

These three points, especially the last two, are infallible reference marks.

The meeting of the *head line* and the *line of Fatality* is 20 years exactly.

The meeting of the *heart line* and the *line of Fatality* is 40 years exactly.

The meeting of the *line of Mercury* or *Apollo* and the *line of Fatality* is 10 or 12 years.

By dividing through the middle these various lines, one obtains the intermediate ages:

30 years at the mid-point between the heart line and the head line (see Figure 11), and likewise for the others.

We do not find these ideas in any of the "classical" books on the question. I guarantee the exactitude of it in 90 cases in 100.

We look, therefore, at whether the line of Fatality is cut and crossed by another line at the level of any one of these points and deduce therefrom the age of an event. So, let us suppose a hand which has the following sign (Figure 10):

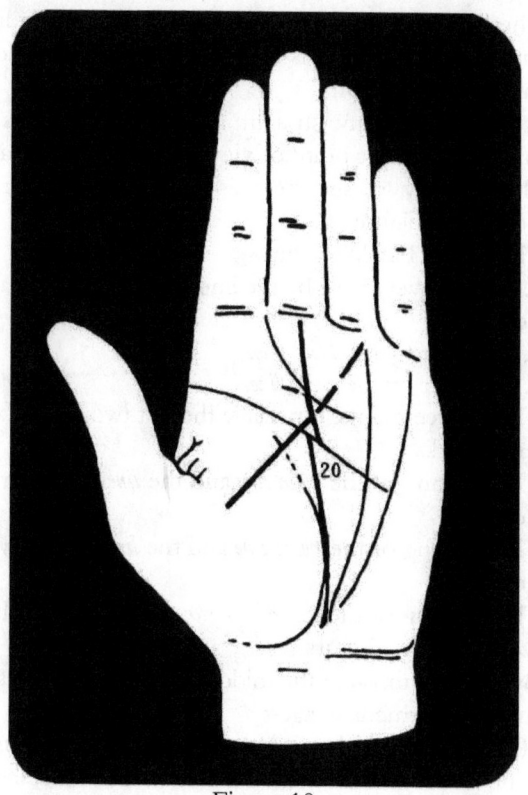

Figure 10
The ages and the events
(*notions unknown by the authors of modern Chiromancy*)

Reading the Signs

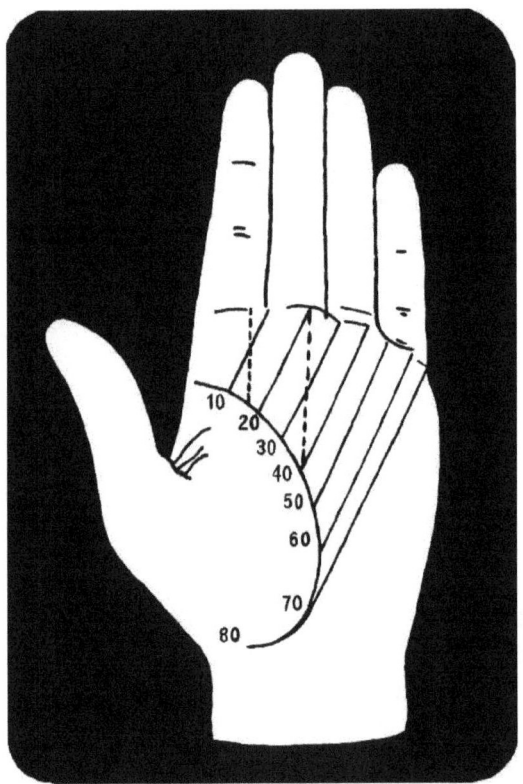

Figure 11
The ages and the life line

Shortly after the twentieth year (meeting of the Saturnian and the head line), the Saturnian makes a leap to the right

You say:

At 20 years old you changed your occupations and you

had the idea to throw yourself into a more intellectual life.

But look at the figure. A line crosses the Saturnian a little after 20 years and directs itself towards Apollo.

You say:

At 20 you decided all of a sudden to occupy yourself with art. From there is a change in all your occupations.

This example developed by practice comes to explain all.

2. ON LUCK (Figure 12)

Luck is indicated by the number of *lines which double* the Saturnian.

Here, then, is a hand which has luck from 20 to 30 years, which loses it from 30 to 40, and which recovers it at 40; but from the point of view of the material position.

Very great luck is indicated by a line doubling the Saturnian for nearly its entire length.

3. ON PHYSICAL LIFE AND ILLNESSES (Figure 13)

Illnesses are seen in the *life line*. I cannot absolutely guarantee the predictions of death at such or such age according to the considerations of this line.

Thus I have examined in the amphitheaters of the hospitals around 200 hands nearly immediately after death, and I have observed the truth of the predictions in only about 60% of the cases.

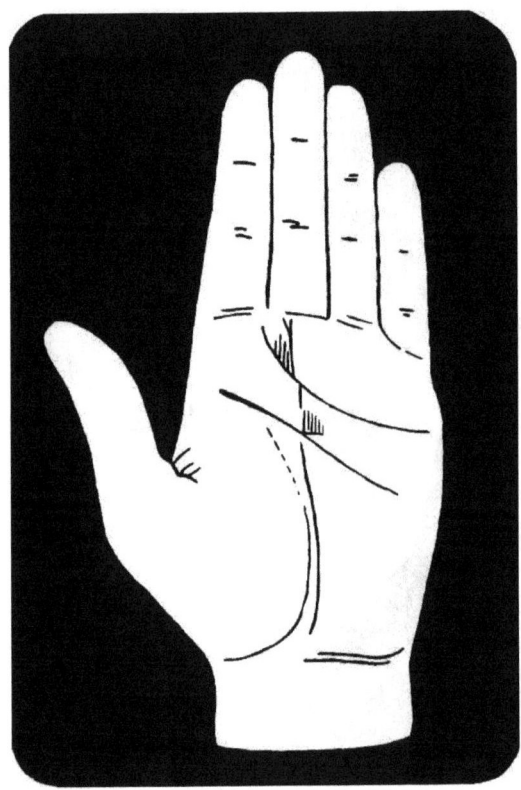

Figure 12
Luck

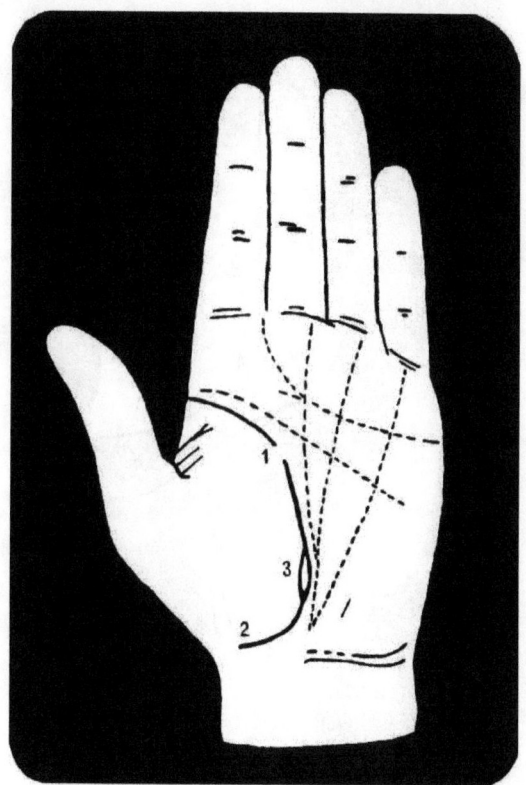

Figure 13
Some indications on the life line

It is necessary, therefore, to corroborate the teachings of the life line with those of the line of Fatality, and especially by the examination of both hands.

The ages are thus indicated in this line (we will find in the treatise of Desbarolles the key of this division).

A grave illness from which one recovers is marked by an interruption of the life line, followed by the resumption of the line. (See point 1, Figure 13.)

Danger of apoplexy is indicated by the sudden stopping of the line without resuming.

Illnesses of languor are marked by a continued weakening of the life line which becomes at the end so thin that one may hardly follow it.

Paralyses are, in general, indicated by iles. (See point 3, Figure 13.)

4. ON THE EGO

The thumb indicates man himself and his triple division:

- *Head* or superior phalanx;
- *Chest* or median phalanz;
- *Abdomen* or Thenar Eminence (the fleshy eminence in which the thumb originates).

The character of the individual is seen in the superior phalanx. A passionate person has this phalanx nearly squared; a generous person has the phalanx turned out.

A superior phalanx of the thumb that is very large and very thick in comparison to the rest of the digit indicates a dreadful character being able to go to the point of *assassination*.

One recounts that Lacenaire was long followed in his life by Vidocq who believed in chiromancy and who had found in him the thumb of an assassin.

All these details are found set forth very well in the known books dedicated to this question.

Let us recall that the ancients considered the thumb as a symbol of the man himself to such a degree that they cut the thumb of the cowards; from this the word *poltroon* (cut thumb, *pollice trunco*).

5. ON SENSUAL LOVE (Figure 14)

The ideal love is indicated in the *heart line*.

Sensual love in the Mound of Venus.

The passing loves are marked by little lines, numerous and not very deep (point 2).

The serious loves by the deep lines. There may be only one sole love in life (point 1).

The tendency towards lasciviousness is indicated by grids at the base of the Mound of Venus (point 3).

6. MARRIAGE OF LOVE (Figure 14)

The marriage of love is indicated by a cross under Jupiter (point 4).

The cross badly formed indicates that the marriage on the point of being made is not concluded.

When an accessory bar crosses the cross below, it indicates very great obstacles to the marriage.

7. ON THE WILL (Figure 15)

The will is marked by the depth of the *head line* which also indicates courage.

Physical wounds which depend on Mars are also indicated on this line by points.

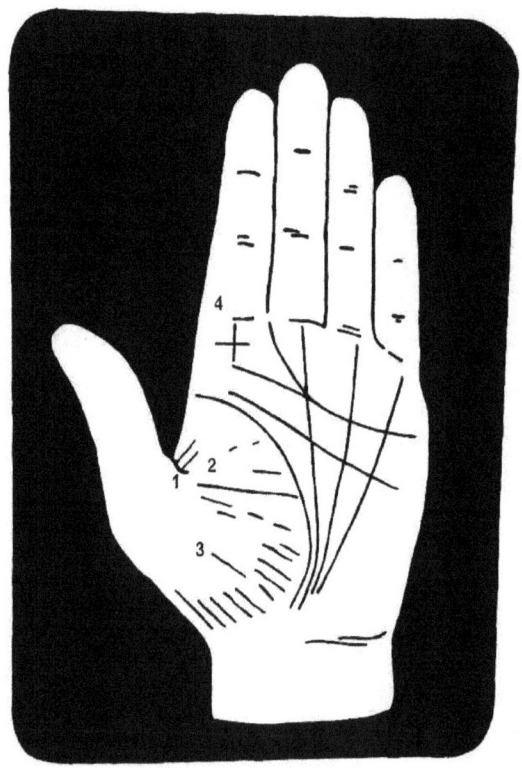

Figure 14
Love

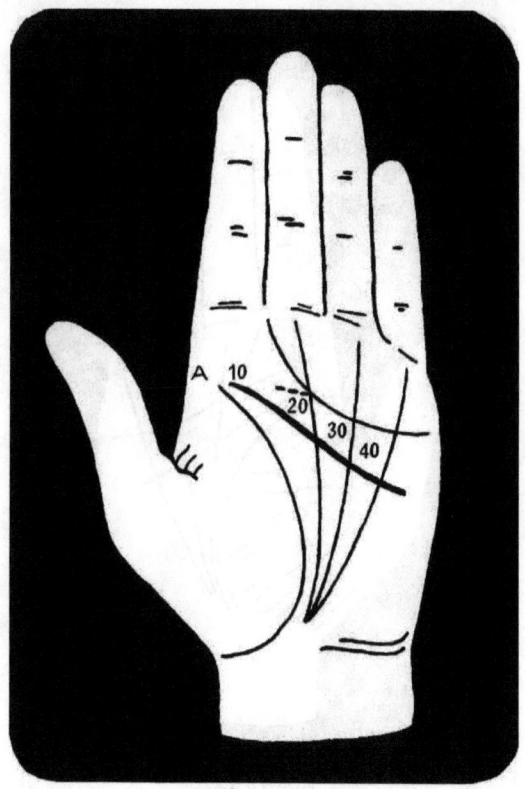

Figure 15
The ages of the head line
(lines of Mars unknown by the moderns)

The ancient treatises on chiromancy from the 16th century divide this line into ages in order to indicate the events.

The meeting of the *Saturnian* and this line is at 20 years

old.

The meeting of the *line of the Sun* with it is at 40.

The meeting of the *Mercurial* is at 60 years; Phillipe May has given an equivalent division. The perpendiculars dropped from the middle of this root of the medius is 25 years; from the middle of the root of the ring finger is 50 years; from the middle of the root of the little finger is 73 years. (Figure 16.)

8. ON AUDACITY AND SUCCESS

An important remark to make, and the one by which one ought to begin the observation of all hands, is that:

When the *head line* and the *life line* are separated from one another, the individual has an unshakable confidence in his star and in himself, and he will succeed in nearly all that he will undertake.

When the lines are united by little intermediary lines, the individual has confidence in his star, but not in himself.

When the lines are exceedingly united, the individual is always desolate, has no confidence in anything, and fails in the majority of undertakings.

9. ON THE SENTIMENTAL LIFE (Figure 17)

The passions of sentimental source, moral grief, and ideal love, are indicated by the *heart line* (line of Jupiter).

The more this line is marked, the more the individual is generous and magnanimous, the more he is susceptible to self-sacrifice, the more he has heart.

We can see the era of great mental grief by the divisions of this line or the crosses that it contains, and by considering the ages which are marked therein.

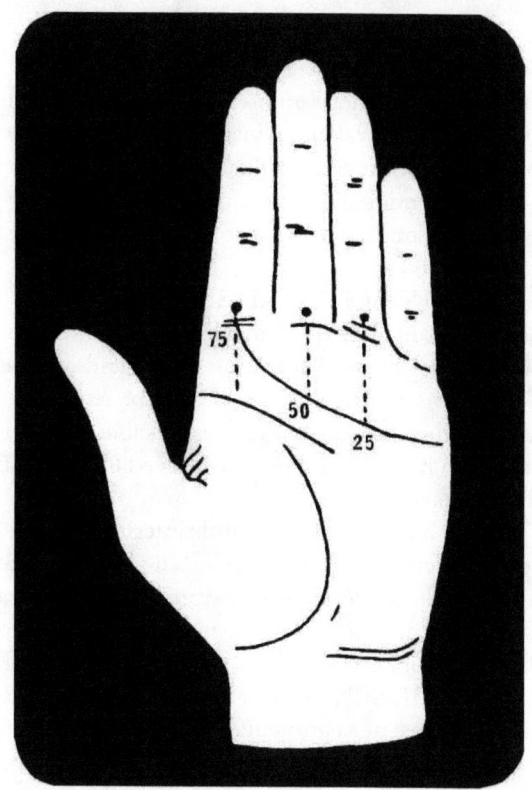

Figure 16
Equivalent system by Philippe May

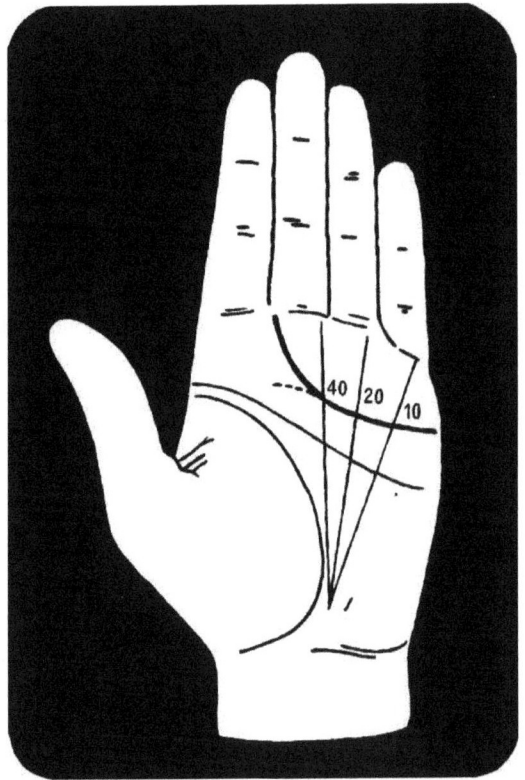

Figure 17
The ages of the heart line
(unknown to the moderns)

The meeting of the *Mercurial* and the *heart line* is 10 or 12 years.

The meeting of the *heart line* and that of *Apollo* is 20 years.

The meeting with the Saturnian is 40 years.

One will find the details on this line in all the treatises on chiromancy.

10. ON ART - ON FORTUNE (Figure 18)

The length of the line of Apollo indicates the faculty to invent or to idealize.

When this line is accompanied by a multitude of other small lines under the finger of Apollo, the individual has very developed artistic tendencies (point A).

Musicians usually have a number of small lines slightly marked; poets or painters have fewer lines, but deeper.

A fork at the top of this line indicates fortune (point B).

11. ON SCIENCE (Figure 19)

The line of Mercury accompanied by small lines under the little finger indicates the taste for science (and not specially for medicine, as says Desbarolles).

One will see the kind of science by the existence or non-existence of the *line of intuition* continuing itself in the hand.

Just as the thumb become pernicious indicated the assassination, the spatulate little finger, that is to say materialized and terminating in a *club* (see the works of d'Arpentigny) indicates the tendency *towards theft*, pet sin of the god Mercury who receives at the same time the homage of merchants and thieves.

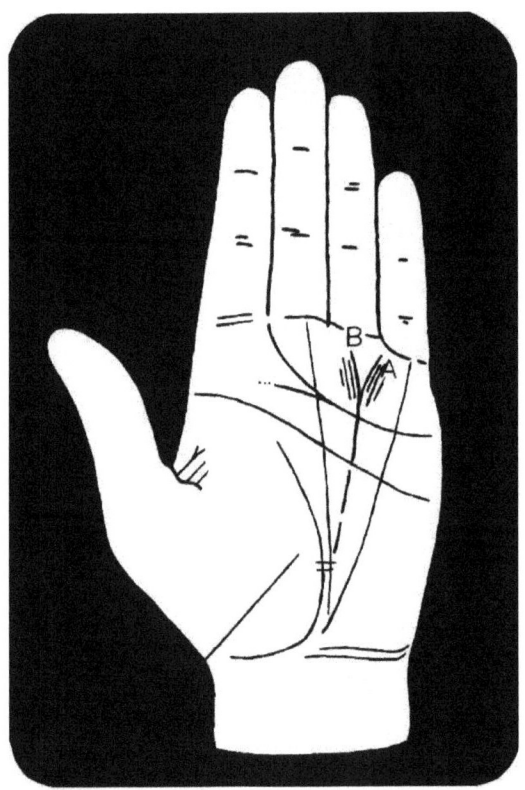

Figure 18
Art and fortune

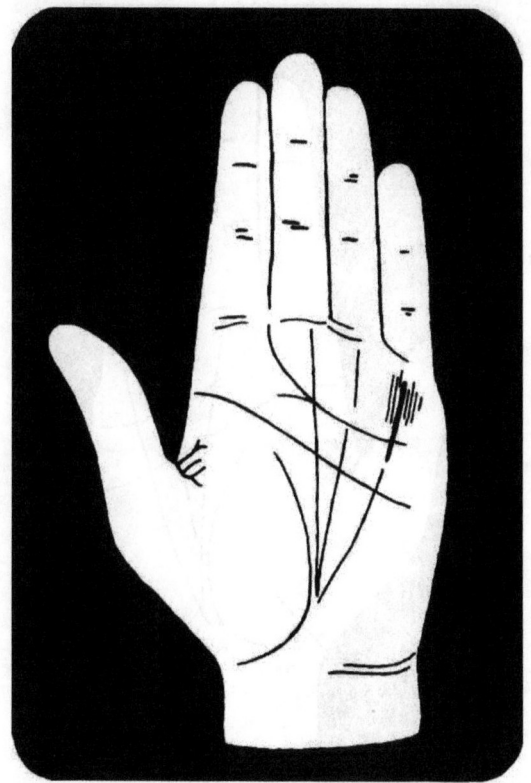

Figure 19
Science

12. ON COMMERCE

One single deep line under Mercury indicates the taste for commerce.

13. TASTE FOR GLORY OR MONEY (Figure 20 and 21)

The ideal of the theorist is glory.

The ideal of the practical man is money.

In order to see at once which one of his tastes dominates among an individual, one looks at which one of the fingers, index or ring finger, is taller than the other. This comparison is very easy, thanks to Saturn.

If the ring finger (Apollo) is taller, it is that the love of glory outweighs the love of money, and that one prefers in general the ideal to the practical life.

The contrary takes place if Jupiter is taller than Apollo.

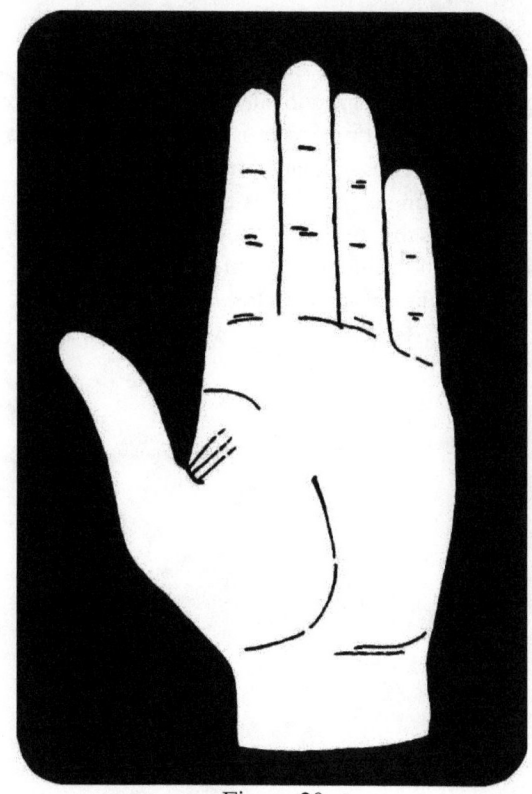

Figure 20
Love of glory (intuitive)

Reading the Signs

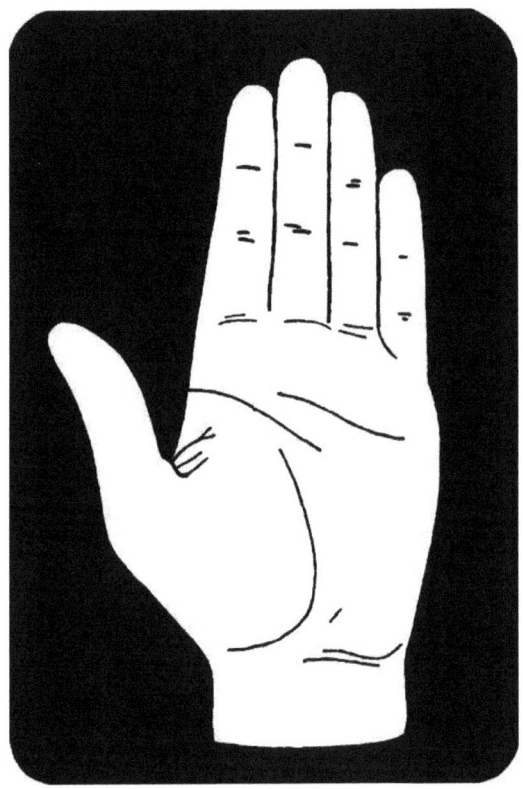

Figure 21
Love of money (deductive)

SECOND PART
Analytical Chiromancy

Some words on the History of Chiromancy

In the initiatic sanctuaries of antiquity, all the sciences were restored, by the union of Metaphysics with Mathematics, in a luminous and profound synthesis. The scission between the sciences of the Spirit and those of nature broke the original Mathèse[3] and, from that time, began that scientific anarchy which would end in the passing triumph of materialism. Astrology was separated from Astronomy, Alchemy from Chemistry, Hermeticism from Medicine, Physiognomy from Anatomy, and Magic from Physics. The whole portion of the Mathèse that was truly spiritual and luminous became, under the name of Occult Sciences, *a collection of so-called mystical theories which they removed with horror, while the other portion of the Mathèse, the material and obscure portion, became, under the name of* Exact Sciences *of observation, a collection of knowledge to which the modern generations of seekers dedicate their intelligence. But the metaphysical or occult sciences were no longer studied but by some bold innovators who were, moreover, considered by their adversaries as charlatans or as unbalanced.*

The deductive and intuitive Sciences of divination were even divided to infinity, through the succession of the ages; and divination by the inspection of the human being was portioned into a multitude of sections: divination by the shape of the features, or physiognomy; divination by the lines inscribed upon the face (and in particular on the forehead) or metoposcopy; divination by the lines of the hand, or chiromancy, etc., etc...

Divination by the lines of the hand, or chiromancy, underwent in its turn various transformations.

Originally attached to the Hermetic sciences in the medical section, chiromancy was purely astrological.

Later (14th, 15th, 16th centuries), with this astrological chiromancy came to be mingled an elementary translation for the people, in which there was no planetary name: chiromancy was purely physical.

Finally, in the 19th century, shortly after the transformation carried out by Gall *in physiognomy by the study of the bumps of the head, the captain d'Arpetigny modified chiromancy considerably by the study of the shape of the fingers, or chirognomy. Finally, some contemporary seekers, among whom we cite Mr. Louis Mond, posed the bases of a comparative chiromancy, or study of the relationship between the shape of the hands and its lines with the face or with the writing.*

The majority of the contemporary authors, not bothering to make these distinctions, make a hotch-potch of all these systems in which chirognomy, of recent creation, goes along side of traditional astrological chiromancy, itself obscured by physical chiromancy. And the dumbfounded reader no longer knows how to recognize oneself in these details as multifarious as poorly laid out.

CHAPTER III
Division to establish in the study of the hand

The study of the hand is a true science for the chiromancer. This study has need, therefore, to be portioned into several sections which facilitate its comprehension.

The practitioner notes first that the hand is formed of three principal segments:

- 1. Its attachment to the forearm: the *wrist*.
- 2. The center of implantation of the fingers and the very base of the hand: the *palm*.
- 3. The articulated organs which radiate around the palm: the *fingers*.

The aim that the chiromancer pursues is the knowledge of the connections which may exist between the indications furnished by the hand and the fatal or voluntary impulse that the individual undergoes. To determine these indications, the artist will study successively:

- 1. The SHAPE of the hand, its CONSISTENCY, its COLOR, etc., in the three divisions of wrist, palm, and fingers. That is to say that one will study successively the indications furnished by the shape or consistency of the palm, by the shape or consistency of the fingers, etc...

This is the section denominated *Chirognomy*.

- 2. After the shape, the artist will approach the study of the LINES which streak through the shapes.

This is the section denominated *Chiromancy* proper.

- 3. After having considered the teachings furnished by the shape and lines of the hand, the artist, elevating himself even higher, will research the raison d'être of these shapes and these lines, from where he will deduce the relationship existing between the hand and the face,-between the hand and writing, etc., etc.

This will be the section concerning the Philosophy of the hand or *Chirosophy*.

We see, then, that the term *Chiromancy*, by which we designate generally the study of the hand, does not correspond to all the divisions of the hand, nor to all the divisions of this art; but as this term comprises the section most anciently studied, it is permitted to preserve it to denominate the whole, but while making the necessary distinctions.

If one now notes that the description, the analysis, and the synthesis thus specified ought to successively approach the study of the three parts of the hand: wrist, palm, and fingers, one will see that there exists:

A Chirognomy ⎤
A Chiromancy ⎬ of the wrist
A Chirosophy ⎦
A Chirognomy ⎤
A Chiromancy ⎬ of the palm
A Chirosophy ⎦
A Chirognomy ⎤
A Chiromancy ⎬ of the fingers
A Chirosophy ⎦

All is synthesized in astrological or comparative Chirosophy - by which Chiromancy is attached to the other sciences of divination.

CHAPTER IV
On the study of the shapes, or Chirognomy

One may arrive, by the simple inspection of the various parts of the hand, at some most precise determinations, concerning the character and the aptitudes of any person whatsoever. But we will not obtain by this means any indication concerning the events which have acted or which may act upon this person. It is therefore very important to delimit, from the outset, the extent of the information furnished by Chirognomy (name given by d'Arpentigny) which corresponds for the hand to the study of the bumps or Phrenology for the head, and to the study of the strokes of Graphology for the Gesture. One is to study successively the shape of the three parts of the hand: 1st, the wrist; 2nd, the palm; 3rd, the fingers, after having rapidly looked at the hand in general.

But beforehand, let us dedicate some words to the brief history of Chirognomy.

The oldest treatises on Chirognomy reserve some paragraphs to the study of the hand in general, considered in its shape, its consistency, and its color. The classical chiromancers of the 16th century all establish the triple division: in wrist, palm, and fingers, which dates from the remotest antiquity. Some occupy themselves with the palm or the fingers; but in a very superficial manner.

It is to captain d'Arpentigny (1863) that we owe the nearly complete creation of this art of Chirognomy, or *art of recognizing the tendencies of the Intelligence according to the shapes of the hand*, as indicates the title of the celebrated work of this author.

On the study of the shapes, or Chirognomy

Desbarolles has later modified the teachings of d'Arpentigny by increasing them; and ever since, all the treatises on Chiromancy contain a section dedicated to Chirognomy. We are going to give to our readers as many extracts as possible from the classical authors.

1. ON THE HAND IN GENERAL

Data furnished by Ronphyle (1665). - The first thing that must be done is to consider the disposition and proportion of the entire hand; for, if it corresponds to the other parts of the human body, it marks a man comprised and endowed with good morals and, on the contrary, if it does not correspond to them, it signifies a man uncomposed and tarnished by some bad habits.

a) Color

It is also necessary to very attentively note the color of the hand, and then to bear its judgment conforming to the nature of the planet to which this color is attributed.

b) Divisions to establish

The table (of the color of the planets and their quality) will be of very great use if the chiromancer, who examines the entire hand, knows prudently and perfectly how to make the connection of the largeness, averageness, or smallness (which are the first differences of the hand), and likewise of the subtlety, bulk, and coarseness (which are the sub-differences of the hand which may agree with each of the preceding differences) with the colors and other qualities of the same hand, such as dryness and humidity; and if he is certain that he will be able to exercise this art with a great facility.

c) The large hand

Generally speaking, the large hand is the sign of a

benevolent and affable man.

Large and slender: marks an ingenious man who values himself.

Large and fleshy: the one who has such a hand is less of an admirer of himself, and if it is found that his hand shows a beautiful color, he will be strongly inclined towards charity and liberality; and furthermore, though he be endowed with a good spirit, it will not be, nevertheless, to the same degree as the one who has hands equally large yet slender, because the latter has more fire than the former.

Large, *thick*, and *rough*: the one who has it in this fashion cannot be but melancholy and, consequently, less affable and less liberal.

It is always necessary to increase or diminish the good or bad omen that one may draw from a hand, according to the good or bad color that it will display.

d) The medium hand

Medium and slender: very subtle Spirit (principally if it is humid).

Medium and fleshy without humidity: marks some difficulty with learning. Yet, if you add therein a pure, sparkling, and clear color, it signifies a man fortunate and destined to dignities and good employment.

Medium, *fleshy*, and *humid*: of blue color, benign, good, and affable man, and somewhat lustful (ruled by Venus and Jupiter).

Id. But of white color, it designates a phlegmatic man (ruled by the Moon).

Id. But of red color: a man proud, liberal, magnificent, and, perhaps scornful of others (ruled by Jupiter and Mars).

Medium, *thick*, and *coarse*: stupid and robust man.

On the study of the shapes, or Chirognomy

e) The small hand

The small hand most often marks a prideful and choleric man.

Small and *slender*: pride, anger, lust, melancholy.

Small, *slender*, and *humid*: diminution of bad influences; ingenious man.

Small, *slender*, and *dry*: joined with some color of Saturn or Mercury, it clearly reveals a man who is thieving, sly, suspicious, and a dreamer.

Small and *fleshy*: the fat weakens the bad omen which arises from the smallness of the hand, and it weakens it all the more when it is accompanied by a more agreeable color and, on the contrary, it diminishes it all the less when it is united with a more [less? - tr.] advantageous color.

f) The bare hand and the hairy hand

Bare hand: effeminate, little inclined towards pleasures of the flesh.

Hairy hand: fickle; not very wise, although very strong.

g) Measure of the proportion of the hand

In order to be proportionate, the hand must contain the following measures:

Measure the distance which separates the middle of the little finger from the middle of the ring finger. You will thus have a length which ought to be contained four times in the breadth of the hand (from the index to the end of the insertion of the little finger), and nine times in the length (from the tip of the medius to the root of the wrist) for a hand fortunate and well-proportioned.

But it is easy to note that this length is equal to that of the second phalanx of the medius, from the first fold to the first adjacent fold, which permits one likewise to take the length of this phalanx as type.

Moreover, in order to be sure that the hand is well proportioned, it is necessary that the distance which separates the middle of the insertion of the index from the middle of the insertion of the little finger is equal to the length of the index from the root to the tip of the finger.

When this proportion is found, this indicates:
1. A man of heart, courageous and virtuous.
2. Good health.
3. A good temperament.

When the proportion is not encountered, this indicates:
1. A proud, base, effeminate, and slothful man.
2. A weak and feeble nature.
3. A bad temperament.

h) Application of these rules to women

When this proportion is encountered among women, it produces there the same effects, and even greater than among men, for it promises them a particular success in their childbirth and, on the contrary, its privation threatens them with extremely painful childbirth, and even sometimes with the danger of death.

When the hand is found larger than it ought to be, it will also have a more important significance and, particularly when it is a question of the spirit of women, this proportion will doubtlessly produce an effect which will not be favorable to her. But when it will be a question of their childbirth, the unequal hands, larger and wider than they ought to be, prognosticates for them more profit than damage, and if it also happens that the triangle is good, it will indicate to a woman that she will be successful in her delivery.

2. ON THE HANDS (According to d'Arpentigny,

1863)

In *large hands*, the *synoptic* spirit, the quibbling and subtle genius, love of polemic, the instinct of controversy; frequently encountered among persons whose *small* and *large hands* join with slender fingers from the knuckles and squared phalanxes.

The very *small slender hands* have *syntheticism*. When they are in the majority of the masses, they are a sign of national decrepitude. Large palms and hard and inert phalanxes preside, on the contrary, over the first developments of the people. They build pyramids, cyclopean enclosures. They worship fetishes.

3. ON THE WRIST

The chirognomy of the wrist is entirely to create. It ought to indicate the relations of a character which unite the consultant with his ancestors. The people, through the study of attachments, aristocratic or not, have posed the first bases of this art, that experience will allow to develop as he merits it.

Those whom this study interests will have to study the relationships which exist between the shape of the fingers and the shape (round, square, or elliptical) of the wrist. It will be necessary, moreover, to see whether the attachment of the hand to the wrist is made by two lines forming an acute angle (fine, aristocratic attachments), an obtuse angle (coarse attachments, simplicity), or whether the two lines remain parallel (straight attachments, energy).

4. ON THE PALM (According to d'Arpentigny)

Too narrow, too slender, too thin, indicates a weak and sterile temperament, an imagination without warmth and without strength, instincts without ability, a taste more delicate than solid, a spirit more subtle than great.

If it is supple, of a suitable thickness and surface, you will be apt to all the pleasures (inappreciable privilege!) and your senses, easily excited, will keep the faculties of your imagination going.

Unless it ceases to be supple, it offers too obvious developments, egotism and sensuality will be your dominant penchants.

Finally, if its width is entirely outside of proportion with the parts of the hand, if it joins with an excessive hardness, and excessive thickness, then it will indicate *instincts* and an individuality marked at the corner by an *animality* without idea.

5. ON THE MOUNDS (Figure 22)

At the level of the root of each finger, as well as at the percussion, the palm presents little fleshy pads called *Mounds* by Chiromancy, and which are developed in a different manner among the various individuals.

At the root of the thumb is the *Mound of Venus*, which indicates all that is related to the family, love, and children.

At the root of the index is the *Mound of Jupiter*, which indicates all that is related to ambition and devotion. - (This is the Mound of the heart).

At the root of the medius is the *Mound of Saturn*, indicating Fatalism and Sadness.

At the root of the ring finger is the *Mound of the Sun* (*Mound of Apollo*), indicating glory and fortune, as well as artistic tendencies.

At the root of the little finger is the *Mound of Mercury*, indicating commerce, medicine, and the natural sciences.

On the study of the shapes, or Chirognomy

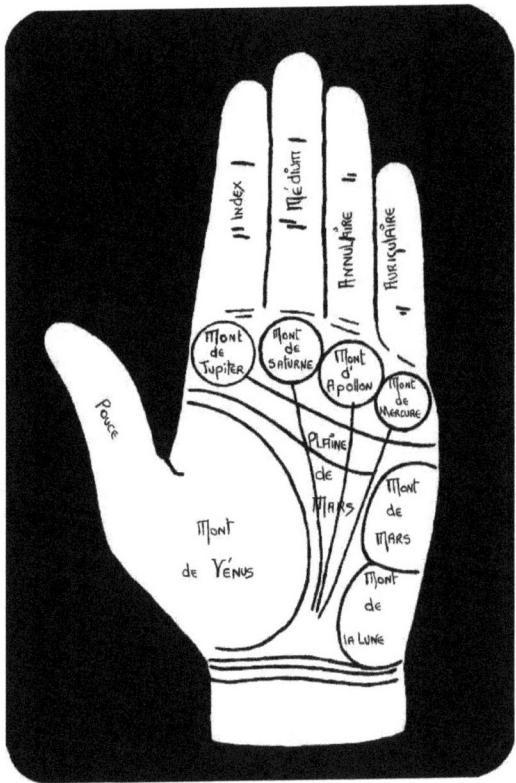

Figure 22
The Mounds

At the percussion of the hand is found at the bottom, on the side of the wrist, the *Mound of the Moon*, which is related to the imagination and water.

Finally, Desbarolles admits a *Mound of Mars* above the *Mound of the Moon*; it is the *Mound of Courage and of the Head*.

6. ON THE FINGERS (Figure 23)

The creator of Chirognomy of the fingers is incontestably d'Arpentigny, who has based nearly his whole system on this study.

Thus, we are going to give some faithful extracts from this author, in a manner to summarize as best we can his work that has become undiscoverable. We will add thereto more figures and remarks which will clarify the passages which could still remain obscure for our readers.

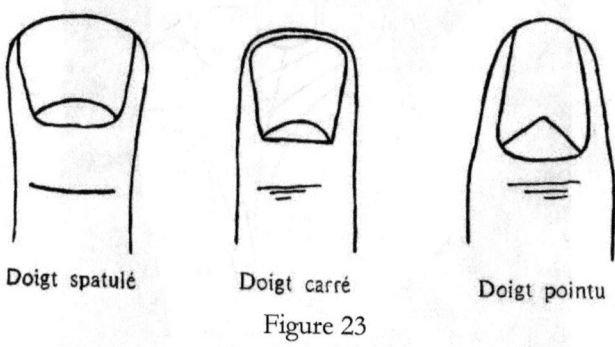

Doigt spatulé   Doigt carré   Doigt pointu

Figure 23

There are smooth fingers, and there are gnarled ones. Among these latter, there are some whose hand has only one knot, others have two. The significant knots are not those that one discovers only with the help of touch; but those that the eye sees first and easily.

Our fingers *terminate* spatulate, that is to say by widening more or less, or squarely, that is to say by a phalanx whose lateral lines are prolonged parallelly, or in a cone, more or less acute.

To these different shapes are attached as many different

signs.

Smooth fingers, even those which terminate *spatulate* or *squarely*, all have more or less ARTISTIC *humor*: so positive is the aim towards which their instinct pushes them, they will proceed always by inspiration rather than by reason, by fantasy and sentiment rather than by knowledge, by synthesis rather than by analysis.

A man spends annually double his income, yet his home, where all is in its place, shines by the arrangement and symmetry. - Smooth fingers with squared phalanx and even spatulate.

a) On the knuckles (Figure 24)

If the knuckle which ties your first phalanx to the second is jutting out, you have order in ideas (A); if the one which ties your second phalanx to the third is projecting, you have a remarkable dose of material order (B).

The first knuckle never exists without the second; the latter, on the contrary, exists very often without the first.

This implies that the exterior order is always in the faculties of the persons endowed with mental order, whereas a number of people, known for their punctuality, for example, nevertheless have a very illogical mind.

b) The seven typical hands of d'Arpentigny

We have before us seven hands belonging to as many individuals. They are stretched towards us without being supported upon anything, and the fingers partly open.

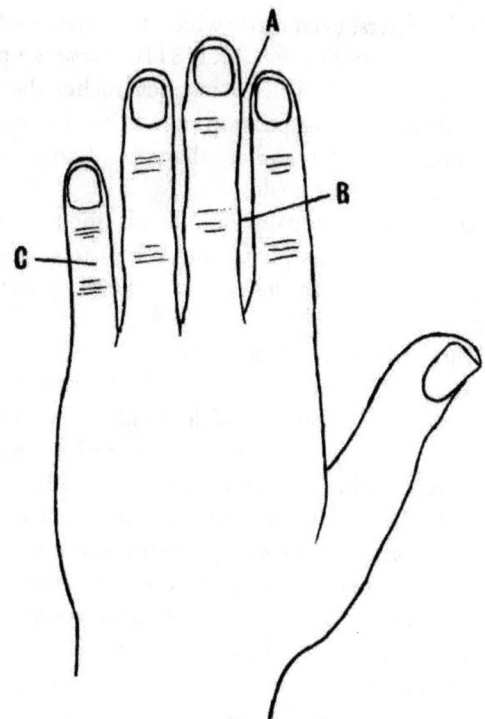

Figure 24
A: philosophical knuckle. - B: material knuckle. - C: smooth finger.

A. - 1st hand: Smooth fingers with spatulate.
2nd hand: Gnarled fingers with spatulate.

The first is furnished with smooth fingers terminating in spatulate.

The second is furnished with gnarled fingers also

terminating in spatulate.

Both of them, *because of the spatulate phalanx*, have imperious need of corporeal agitation, locomotion, and very generally of manual occupation. More guts than brains; the science of *things* by their useful and physically sensible side. Love of horses, dogs, hunting, navigation, war, agriculture, commerce.

Both have an innate sense of tangible things; the instinctive intelligence of *real life*, the veneration of physical strength, the genius of calculation, of the industrial and mechanical arts, the exact applicable sciences, the natural and experimental sciences, the physical arts, administration, law, etc.

Marked aversion for the high philosophical sciences, for transcendent metaphysics, for spiritualist poetry, and even often for any kind of poetry, for subtleties, for all that proceeds from the world of speculative ideas.

Only:

As the *smooth* fingers proceed, as I have just said, by aspiration, passion, instinct, intention, and the gnarled fingers (with double knot) by calculation, reason, deduction, and probabilities, the hands with the *smooth* fingers excel especially in the arts by *locomotion*, in the applicable sciences where spontaneous skill and *impulsive* genius prevail over the combination.

B. - 3rd hand: *Smooth fingers with squared termination.*
      4th hand: *Gnarled fingers with squared termination.*

Both, *because of the squared phalanx*, have the taste for *moral, political, social, and philosophical sciences*; didactic poetry, analytics, drama, grammar, languages, logic, geometry; love of the literary form, meter, rhyme, symmetry, the arrangement, *definite and conventional art*, just views rather than grand ones, genius of business, personal respect, positive and average ideas, instinct of duty and authority, veneration of the *practical* truth, wit, spirit of leadership, love of the progeny, and *generally* more brains than guts.

To the square phalanxes are due the theories, the methods which rule, not the high poetry, it does not reach there, but *literature*, the sciences, and some arts. They carry the name of Aristotle inscribed upon their flag and march at the head of the four faculties.

This type does not shine through the imagination as the poets mean it. Yet what, in the limits which circumscribe it, arises from this faculty, belongs to the smooth fingers, like *literature* proper. I mean that which has only itself for an aim; and what arises from reasoning, from the combination, like the social sciences, history, etc., belong to the gnarled fingers.

Descartes, Pascal had gnarled fingers; Chapelle, Chaulieu had smooth ones.

The spatulate fingers have the action and the *know-how* first, then the *knowledge*; the squared fingers have the *knowledge* first then the *know-how*.

C. - 5th hand: *Smooth fingers with conical termination.*

This fifth hand has smooth fingers whose phalanx offers the shape of a cone or of a sewing thimble.

Plastic arts, painting, sculpture, monumental architecture; poetry of the imagination and of the senses (Aristotle), veneration of the beautiful through the solid and visible form; romantic impulse; antipathy for rigorous deductions; need of *social* independence, propensity towards enthusiasm, tractability towards fantasy.

This same hand with knots: same genius with more combinations and mental strength.

On the study of the shapes, or Chirognomy

D. - 6th hand: *Gnarled fingers with ovoid termination*.

This other hand has gnarled fingers with quasi-squared, quasi-conical phalanxes (the first knuckle giving to the exterior phalanx a nearly ovoid shape).

It indicates a genius turned towards speculative ideas, towards meditation, towards the high philosophical sciences and rigorous deductions *through speech*. Love of absolute truth; poetry of the reason, of the thought, high logic; need of *political*, *religious*, and *social* independence; deism, democracy.

This is the *philosophical hand*.

E. - 7th hand: *Smooth fingers with pointed termination*.

Contemplation, *religiosity*, ideality, unconcern with material interests, poetry of love and of the heart, lyricism, need of life and liberty; veneration of all kinds of beauty, through the form and the essence, but especially through the essence.

I have given to this hand, because of its attributes, the name of *psychic hand*.

c) Summary

Thus, to the spatulate and squared fingers, God has given matter and reality, that is to say industry, the *useful* and *necessary* arts; action, the theory of things, the intelligence of facts, the high sciences.

So, to the conical and pointed fingers, God has opened the limitless field of ideality: giving to the conical fingers the intuition of beauty *according to the exterior sense*, *art*.

To the pointed fingers are given the intuition of the true and beautiful, *according to the inner sense*, high poetry, *idealist philosophy*, *lyricism*.

7. - ON THE THUMB (Figure 25)

"For want of other proofs, the thumb

How to Read Hands

convinced me of the existence of God."
NEWTON

Just as without the thumb, the hand would be a defective and incomplete instrument, so too without *mental* will, logic, decision, and faculties of which the thumb to different degrees offers the different signs, the most fruitful and brilliant spirit would be only a gift without value.

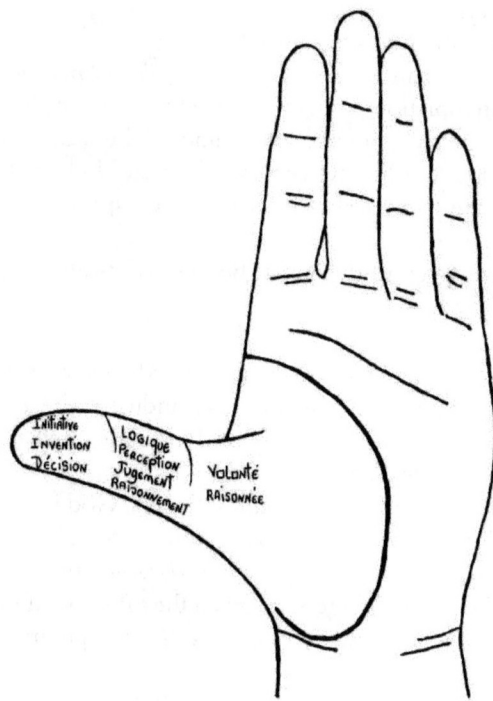

Figure 25

On the study of the shapes, or Chirognomy

In the same way as the animals, we have a will of *instinct*; but the thumb represents only the *reasoned* will, *reasoned* logic, and reasoned decision.

The superior animal is in the hand, man is in the thumb.

Upon the root of the thumb (Mound of Venus of the chiromancers) sits the sign of the *reasoned Will* by which you measure the intensity at the length and thickness of this root. It sheds light therefore, say the chiromancers, on the propensity, more or less, for love. Incidentally, to love is to will, and to will is to love. I will only assert that the sway of the senses is more imperious among small roots than among the large, considering the less reasoned the will, the less mental strength they have.

In the second phalanx is found the sign of logic, that is to say of the perception, judgment, and reasoning.

And in the first, that of invention, decision, and initiative.

Do you have a narrow, slender, thin, and short phalanx? Complete absence of decision, subjection to the opinions received, to the ideas of others, doubt, endless uncertainty, and, in the long run, moral indifference.

This eternal state of your spirit, this incapacity to take a side, you will give a logical explanation for it, if your second phalanx is developed.

You have, on the contrary, fixed ideas, strong and tenacious convictions; you will probably be at the same time a bad reasoner (such a nature is sparing with largess), a man endowed with more mental passion than judgment, if your first phalanx is long and strong; the other, on the contrary, is slender and short.

In general, a small, puny thumb announces an irresolute genius, inconstant, in the things, of course, which arise from the reason, and not from the sentiment or instinct.

People with a small thumb are governed by the heart (thumb of tolerance) and breathes easier in the atmosphere of the sentiments than in that of the ideas. They see better with the *eye of the moment* than with that of reflection.

People with a large thumb are governed by the head (thumb of exclusivity) and breathe easier in the atmosphere of ideas than in that of the sentiments. They see better with the eye of reflection than with the eye of the moment.

8. THE MANNER TO STUDY WELL THE SHAPE OF THE FINGERS

1. Apply the hand upon a large sheet of white paper, large enough to contain this hand, the fingers extended and the palm against the paper.

2. With a sharp pencil, follow very exactly the contour of each finger, while turning around each finger successively.

One will thus have a more faithful and useful tracing of the hand. It will suffice to prolong with a ruler the lines obtained in order to see.

1. *If the fingers are pointed*, then the lines will meet more or less high.

2. *If the fingers are spatulate*, the lines will be removed more and more from one another.

3. *If the lines are square*, the lines will remain parallel.

In the same hand, certain fingers may be spatulate, other square, others pointed. The astrological correspondence then sheds light on the interpretation of each sign.

CHAPTER V
On the study of lines or Chiromancy

The shape indicates, as we have seen, only the tendencies of character. More detailed teachings are going to be furnished to us through the study of the lines.

There are lines on the wrist, there are lines on the palm, there are lines on the fingers. Each of these sections merits a special and detailed study.

1. CAUSE OF THE OBSCURITY OF MANY CLASSICAL TREATISES: THE TWO CHIROMANCIES

When one opens the old treatises on chiromancy, one is surprised to encounter, to designate the lines, names which are far removed from the planetary lines presently employed. It is thus that the Saturnian is called *line of good* or *bad fortune*, the heart or prosperity line and the head line or Natural Mean keep their name; but the line of the Sun is called line of *Wealth or Poverty*. To what owes these different denominations which would seem to indicate, for the ignorant, a disagreement among the Chiromancers?

To the mutual penetration of two systems of Chiromancy: identical by their conclusions, but different by their point of departure; physical Chiromancy and astrological Chiromancy.

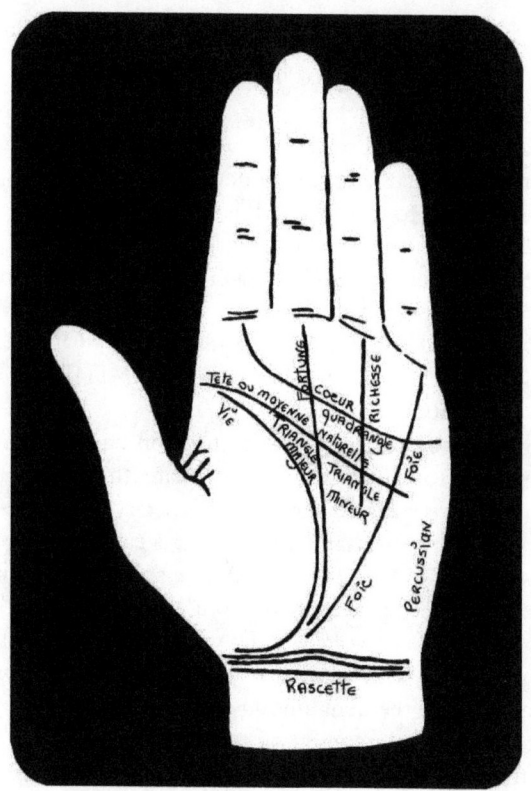

Figure 26
Physical Chiromancy

It is *Physical Chiromancy* which has named the lines: *life*, *head*, *heart*, *wealth*, and *liver* as it has described under the name of *Major Triangle*[5], the space comprised between the Life line, the Saturnian (or Fortune) line, and the Head line; *Minor Triangle*[6], the space comprised between the Saturnian, the Liver (Mercurial) line, and the Head line; *Quadrangle*[7], the space comprised between the Saturnian line, the Liver line on the sides, and the Head and Heart lines at the bottom and top.

In all these names, there is nothing of the planetary or astrological. This seems to be here a translation of the astrological Chiromancy for the use of the people, and it is the system preferred by the Bohemian nomads and little educated fortune-tellers. Whatever the case, this system must be very ancient, and it exercised an undeniable influence over all the works of the chiromancers. But it is a cause of very great obscurity for the reader or young student who gets confused from the first lessons, between the triangles and the Plain of Mars, and who can no longer recognize the lines which bear so many different names. This obscurity disappears as by enchantment when one knows that there are two different systems concurring exactly with the same aim, which leads us to believe that these systems are derived from one another, physical chiromancy being a translation of the other for use by the people.

a) Astrological Chiromancy (Figure 27)

Aside from this physical chiromancy, exists the scientific system whose keys are analogous to those of alchemy or astrology; the chiromancy of influences or *astrological chiromancy*. It is here that we find the origin of the various names given to the lines by popular chiromancy.

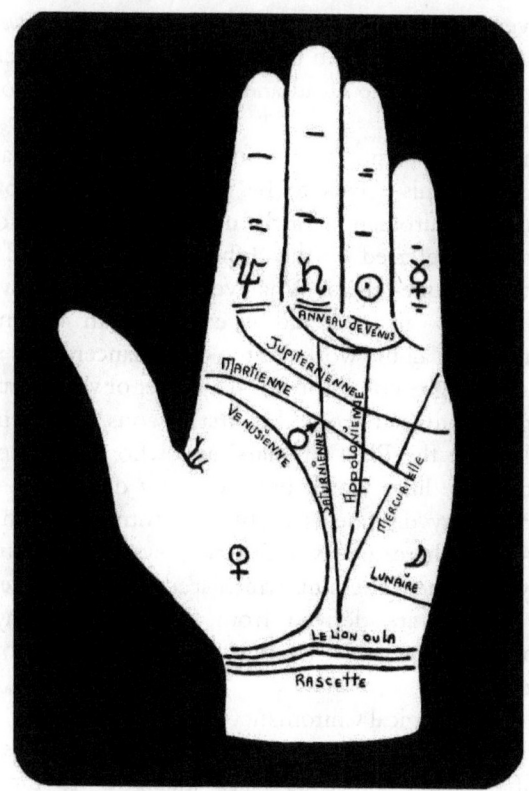

Figure 27
Astrological Chiromancy

Venus presiding over the generation and course of life, the line of Venus has become the *life line*.

Jupiter presided over the grandeur of the soul, over what they call "a good heart"; its line has become the *heart line*, the line of devotion and well-being, the line of Spirit:

the Mensal (*mens*) which indicates the generous side of the cerebral impulses, of which the egotistical side is marked by the line of Mars or of combative reason (*ratio*), the line of the Chief, the *Head line*, the line of reasoning.

It is therefore, not with the vital organs themselves that these lines are especially connected, and the two horizontal lines of the hand indicate well the two different sorts of intellectual impulses to which the human being submits.

1. The altruistic and self-sacrificing impulse; the impulse of the heart ruled by Jupiter.

2. The impulse of egotism and personal domination; the impulse of the head and of calculation ruled by Mars.

Saturn indicated the influence of Destiny in the Human life, its line has become *the line of good and bad fortune*. (Fortune in the sense of Destiny; for it must not be confused with the following.)

Apollo presided over glory and Money; its line becomes the line of *Wealth or Poverty*.

Mercury, god of Medicine, finds itself attributed to a line of the *liver or stomach*.

Thus, the simplistic translation of the astrological notions has allowed the creation of physical chiromancy, which would, eventually, so confuse the technical treatises.

It suffices to re-establish the astrological meaning of each line, according to the planet on which it depends, in order to return to an interpretation at once clear and rational.

See Figure 27 which, compared to the previous, will allow one to grasp the origin of all the obscurities of the classical authors.

b) Tradition and experience

The given facts concerning chiromancy draw their origin from two principal sources.

1. *Tradition*, which poses the problems to resolve, and whose origin is as ancient as that of the Occult Science itself; that is to say that one encounters this tradition in its fundamental lines back to the primitive civilizations of India.

2. *Experience*, which controls the ideas of the tradition by the study of the connections which exist between the chiromantic lines and the past experiences of the individual, and which draws from there deductions for the future.

Each chiromancer has therefore brought to the tradition notions drawn from his own experience, and the contemporary seekers, who occupy themselves with chiromancy in a truly serious and scientific fashion, have borne their efforts upon the experimental unification of the teachings of the tradition.

After these preliminary clarifications, it seems to us useless to approach the history of chiromancy proper, which could only be a sort of bibliographical biography, since the authors have passed, successively across the ages, the notions of the tradition enriched by their personal discoveries. It is to Desbarolles that is due the greatest credit form this point of view, and his works will always remain as models of the genre.

Faithful to the classical division, that certain authors have wrongly not followed methodically, in its details, we are going to study successively:

- The Chiromancy of the Wrist.
- The Chiromancy of the Palm (the most important).
- The Chiromancy of the Fingers.

We will first rapidly describe the lines, and then we will return to the details.

2. CHIROMANCY OF THE WRIST (Figure 28)

We notice on the wrist a series of lines which, according to the tradition, are related to the age and to family events. The ensemble of these lines is called the rascette (these lines are sometimes called the *restricted* "restrictæ") and are connected astrologically to the zodiacal Lion.

Moreover, the following extracts will indicate the different phases of the tradition in the various epochs.

"*On the Rascettes and the Restricted.* - These lines begin under the Mountain of Venus and end under that of the Moon. This first is called *Rascette*, and all the following *Restricted.*"

May de Franconne (chap. XIV).

"The restricted or rascettes are thus named either because they limit and thus, so to speak, restrict the hand; or because they are restricted and limited to the small space in the narrowest part of the hand."

Ronphyle, p. 36.

"Look at whether a line goes from the restricted to the percussion of the hand, it is a sign of bad fortune or unhappiness. If this line goes from the restricted to the mountain of Jupiter, that is to say towards the index, this signifies that you will not live in your country and that you will go far away to finish your days."

Balsamo (*Myst. de la Destinée*, p. 66)

How to Read Hands

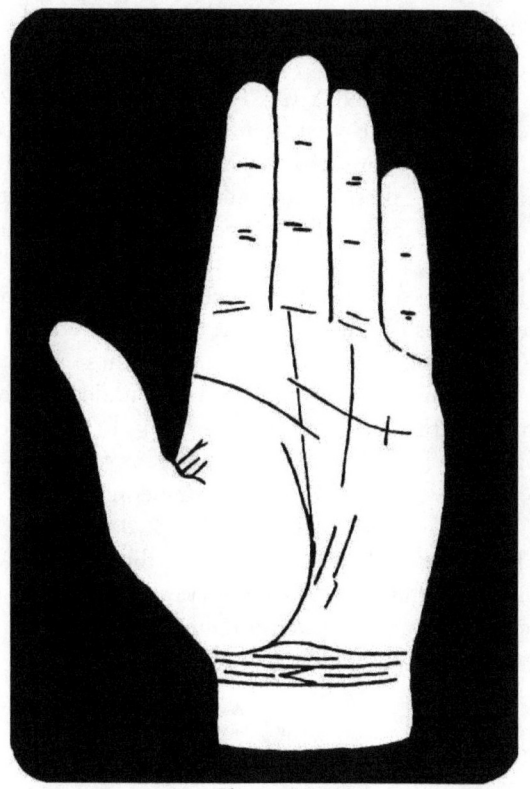

Figure 28
The rascette and the restricted

"These lines, in Chiromancy, each signify twenty-five to thirty years of existence. Three beautiful lines, well traced, form what they call in ancient Chiromancy the magic bracelet, that is to say health and wealth. I add less importance than the ancients to the perfection of this· sign;

but nevertheless, it is a very fortunate prognostic, especially if the hand is intelligently and energetically disposed. The ancients claimed that if there is found a cross in the middle of the lines of the rascette, there is an inheritance. As many inheritances as crosses. These signs are generally realized in my experience: but I do not yet know whether I ought to give them as infallible; yet, I believe it very advantageous to have in the lines of the rascette a cross thus disposed.

"However, it is certain that a line which departs from the rascette without touching it absolutely and which, while crossing the entire hand, ascends the Mound of the Sun, announces a most brilliant success, either in honor or in fortune; sometimes even in fortune and in honor."

Desbarolles
(*Révélat. complètes*, p. 151)

"The wrist with the Lion has the power of the true secret and indicates conjugal happiness.

"When an angle is formed towards the superior part facing the thumb, it is the certain sign of an inseparability, despite the little love which exists between the two spouses.

"When a cross in the Mound of the Moon sends all its strength towards the arm at the opposite of the thumb, it indicates death by shipwreck.

"If it represents an oval sign, or that the first two lines which are marked on the wrist are rejoined at the two extremities, this is a most favorable sign, for it foretells numerous successions, and one will have a respectable fortune from childhood."

Marie Burlen
(*L'arc-en-ciel*, p. 216 and following)
1894.

1. CHIROMANCY OF THE PALM OF THE

HAND

The palm of the hand is streaked with lines whose name we have indicated ahead of this work in our first two lessons on Synthetic Chiromancy.

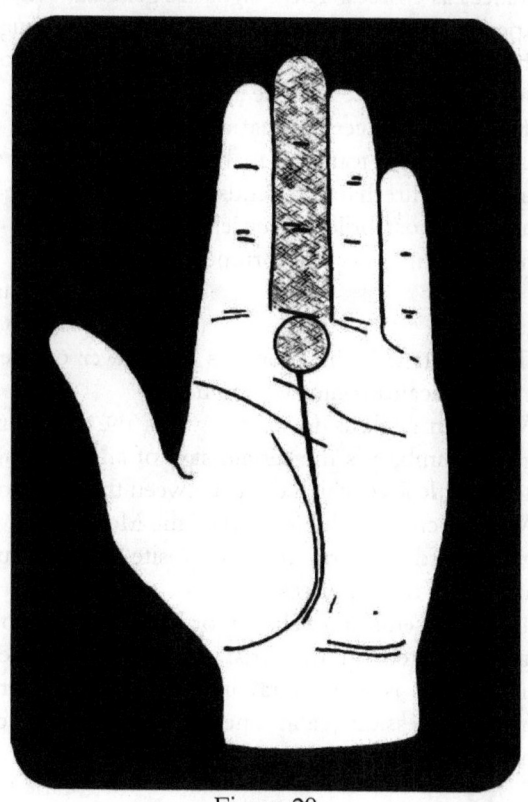

Figure 29
Saturn

We will recall the composite figure and we will approach the study of each line in its principal details. We will lay stress on the different names given to the lines, in a manner to allow our readers to find their way again in the denominations used by the different authors.

a) The line of Saturn or line of Fatality (See likewise Figure 2)

- *Denominations*: Saturnian. Liver line. Line of good or bad fortune. Line of well-being or of Saturn.

- *Situation*: Placed under the medius, which it prolongs vertically.

- *Course*: Begins towards the second half of the life line and goes towards the Mound of Saturn, where it generally ends, and which may be more or less included in its course.

- *Connections*: Departing from the life line, cuts successively: 1st, the head line or line of Mars; 2nd, the heart line or line of Jupiter.

- *Is influenced* directly by Venus and the Moon below, by Mars in the middle, by Jupiter on top, and indirectly by Mercury.

- *Indications*: Good or bad destiny. All that is fatal in our existence (and yet which our will can modify if we have a firm intention). - The events and changings of position.

- *Ages indicated*: At the meeting of the head line: 20; at the meeting of the heart line, 40 years.

b) The line of Jupiter or heart line (See likewise Figure 5)

- *Denominations*: Mensal. Heart line, Line of the entrails. Mensal or fortune. Line of happiness.

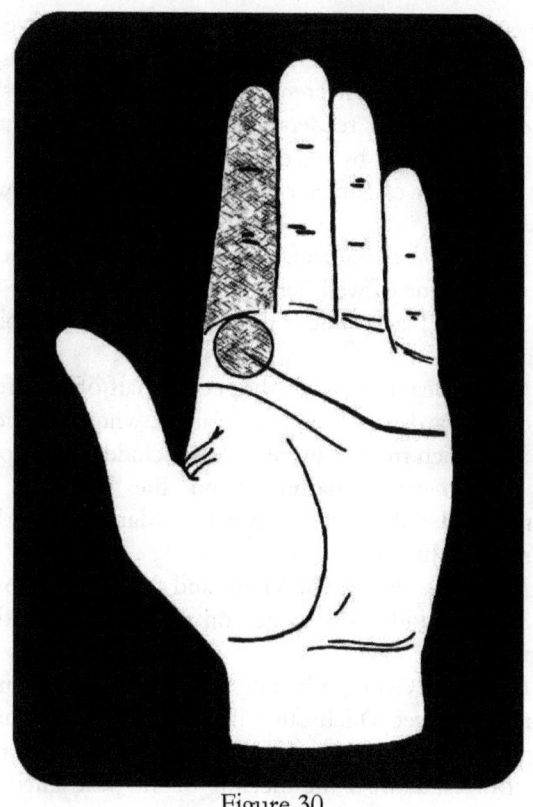

Figure 30
Jupiter

- *Situation*: The first large horizontal line after the root of the fingers.
- *Course*: Begins under the little finger and goes towards the index which it reaches more or less completely.
- *Connections*: Cuts successively: 1st, the line of Mercury;

2nd, the line of Apollo; 3rd, the line of Saturn.

- *Is influenced* directly by Mercury, by Apollo, and by Saturn at the top; indirectly by the Moon and Mars at the bottom.

- *Indications*: Moral life and well-being, self-sacrifice or egotism. All the feminine qualities, or those of the heart.

- *Ages indicated*: (See Figure 16).

c) The line of Mars or head line (See likewise Figure 7)

- *Denominations*: Natural line or line of the brain. Head line. Line of the chief. Natural mean. Line of health or spirit. Line of the spirit.

- *Situation*: The second large horizontal line under the fingers, intermediary between the line of Jupiter or heart line and the line of Venus or life line (from here its name, for some authors, of "Natural Mean").

- *Course*: Begins at the root of the thumb at the same point as the life line and goes towards the percussion of the hand.

- *Connections*: Cuts successively: 1st, the Saturnian; 2nd, the line of Apollo; 3rd, the line of Mercury.

- *Is influenced* directly by Venus, Mars, and the Moon; indirectly by Jupiter, Saturn, and Apollo; very little by Mercury.

- *Indications*: Intellectual life and the spirit. Reasoning or ignorance. All the masculine qualities, or those of the head.

- *Ages indicated*: (See Figure 15).

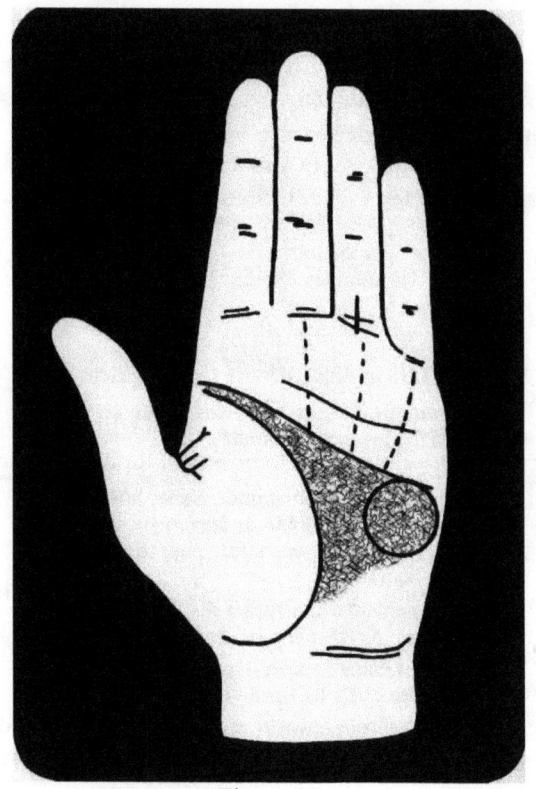

Figure 31
Mars

d) The line of Apollo, of the sun, or line of wealth (See likewise Figure 4)

- *Denominations*: Line of Apollo. Line of the Sun. Line of wealth or poverty.
- *Situation*: Under the ring finger, which it prolongs

vertically.

- *Course*: Begins more or less clearly under the life line and rises vertically towards the Mound of Apollo.

- *Connections*: Cuts successively: 1st, sometimes the line of Saturn at its beginning; 2nd, the head line; 3rd, the heart line.

- *Is influenced* directly by Venus and Mars at the bottom, by Mercury and Saturn at the top. Indirectly by the Moon at the bottom, by Jupiter at the top.

- *Indications*: Art, glory, and fortune; wealth or poverty.

e) The line of Venus or life line (See likewise Figure 6)

- *Denominations*: Vital. Life- line. Line of Venus. Heart line.

- *Situation*: Surrounds the thumb at its root, the third large horizontal line in proceeding from the fingers.

- *Course*: Begins on the index to the root of the thumb which it turns around until the wrist.

- *Connections*: At the beginning with the start of the line of Mars or head line, at the bottom and often in connection with the beginning of the lines of Saturn and Mercury, at the end with the rascette (line of the wrist).

- *Is influenced* directly by Venus and Mars, indirectly by Jupiter at the start of irs course and by the Moon at the end; very little by Saturn and Apollo on the one side, by Mercury on the other.

- *Indications*: Health and character. Generation and the family. All that concerns marriage or celibacy, parents or children.

- *Ages indicated*: (See Figure 11).

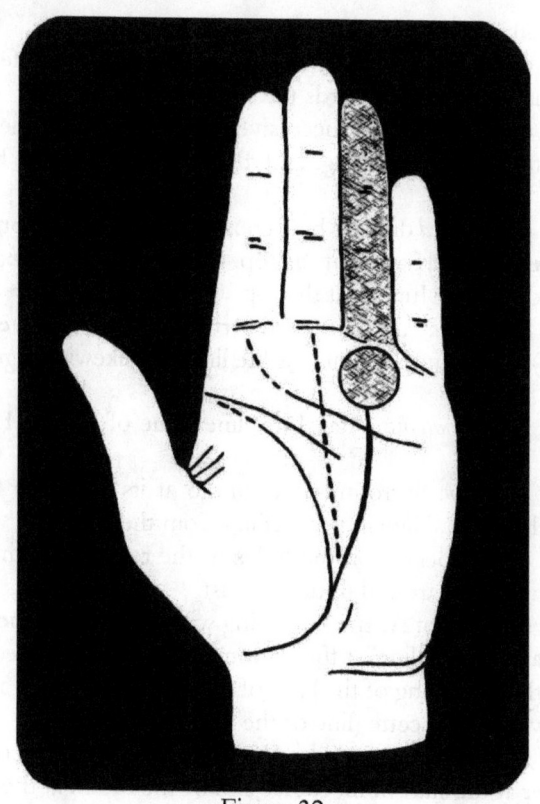

Figure 32
Apollo

On the Study of lines or Chiromancy

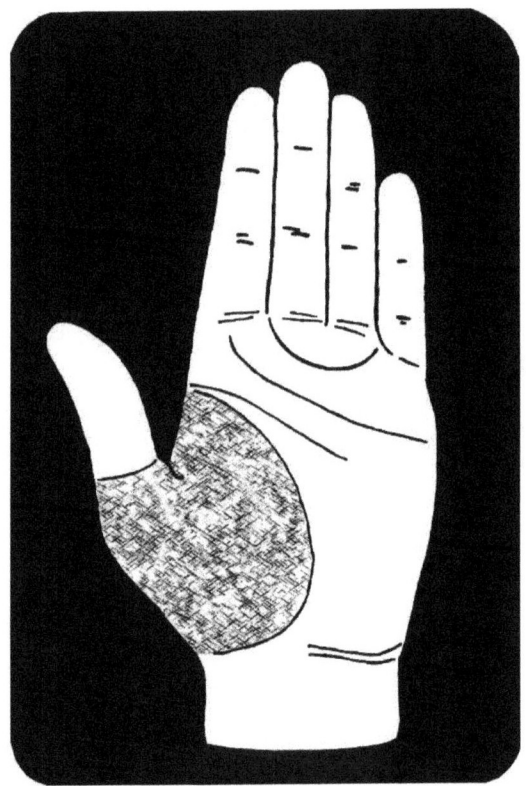

Figure 33
Venus

f) The line of Mercury or hepatic line (See likewise Figure 3)

- *Denominations*: Line of Mercury. Milky Way. Hepatic line. Line of the lung, liver, stomach. Liver line.
- *Situation*: Under the little finger which it promongs

vertically and a little obliquely.

- *Course*: Generally begins at the same point as the Saturnian and goes towards the Mound of Mercury.

- *Connections*: Cuts successively: 1st, the head line; 2nd, the heart line.

- *Is influenced* by the Moon at the bottom, by Apollo at the top; indirectly by Venus and Mars at the bottom, by Saturn at the top; very little by Jupiter.

- *Indications*: Finesse. Presentiment. Intuition.

- *Ages indicated*: Meeting of the Martian, 25 years; of the Jupiterian, 50 years.

g) The ring of Venus (Figure 33)

The ring of Venus, situated above the heart line between the Mounds of Jupiter and Apollo, indicates physical love in all its modalities. Broken, it is, according to tradition, a sign of perversion.

On the Study of lines or Chiromancy

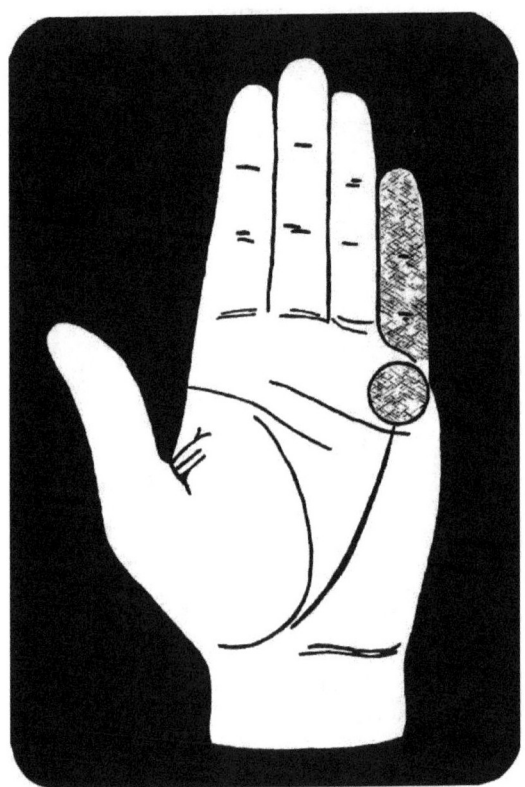

Figure 34
Mercury

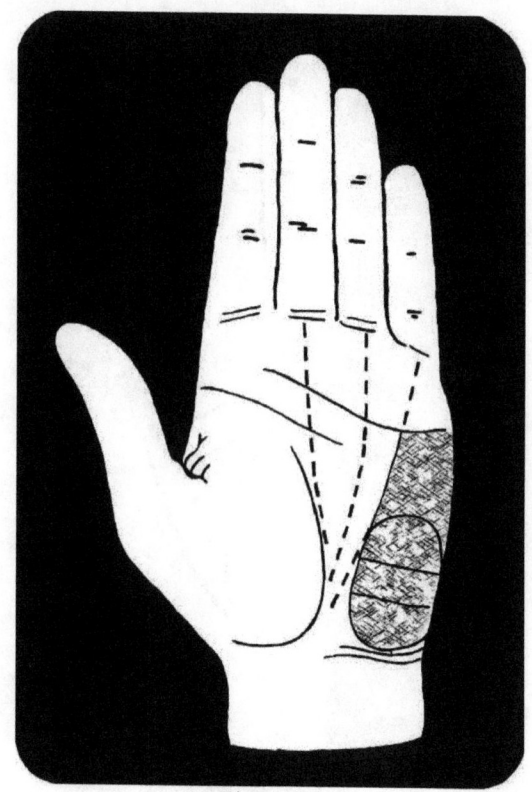

Figure 35
The Moon

4. CHIROMANCY OF THE FINGERS
a) The thumb (man)
- *First phalanx*: A star. Very good sign. Prosperity.
- *Second phalanx* (with nail): A cross. Poverty.
b) The index

- First phalanx of the index (following the mound): Horizontal lines indicating inheritance. A large vertical line ending with a star, large inheritances.

ASTROLOGICAL RELATION: May (Gemini).

Two parallel lines being cut with two others indicates adultery.

- Second phalanx of the index: Horizontal lines indicate envy and falsehood. Vertical and parallel lines, children.

ASTROLOGY: *April*, Taurus.

- Third phalanx (with nail) of the index:

ASTROLOGY: *March*, Aries.

c) The little finger (*Mercury*)

- First phalanx: An M indicates an orator.

ASTROLOGY: *November*, Sagittarius.

- Third phalanx (with nail): A cross indicates extreme poverty.

ASTROLOGY: *September*, Libra.

d) The ring finger (*Apollo*)

- First phalanx: ASTROLOGY: *August*, Virgo.

- Second phalanx: ASTROLOGY: *July*, Leo.

Vertical lines indicate great honors, but little money.

- Third phalanx (with nail): June Cancer.

Small vertical lines in the hand of a woman indicate wealth by the death of a husband.

e) The medius (*Saturn*)

- First phalanx: ASTROLOGY: *February*, Pisces.

- Second phalanx: ASTROLOGY: *January*, Aquarius.

Grill marks destroy the inauspicious influence of Saturn.

- Third phalanx (with nail): ASTROLOGY: *December*, Capricorn.

A cross indicates sterility for a woman.

5. CHIROMANCY OF THE NAILS

Mr. Ernest Bose has published a reprint of the works on chiromancy by Philippe May de Franconie. One reads there a treatise on the marks of the mails in which our readers will find curious details. Some short extracts will indicate the character of this treatise.

When one has a longing to know something of the future, and the month, week, and day when it will occur, it is necessary to seek this out in the nails of the fingers which have the property to indicate it.

Firstly, each nail grows from the root to the end in three months. This is why when a sign begins to appear and grow close to the root, it reaches its course only in the term of three months, in which space it will produce its effect, unless it is impacted by other unfortunate signs.

Here is the manner of operation.

Each nail is divided into three parts:

1. Near the root, a white part in which issue forth the signs. This part indicates what will happen in four weeks. It is the future.

2. The middle of the nail indicates the present and also includes four weeks.

3. The end of the nail at the top indicates the past and also includes four weeks.

That said, let us look at how the signs must be interpreted.

On the Study of lines or Chiromancy

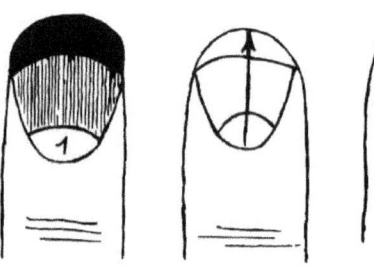

Figure 37
The marks of the nails

1. The *white* signs are good, the *black* or colored signs are bad. The *deep pits* are extremely bad.
2. The normal route of a sign is the middle of the nail, or a vertical path. (See Figure 37 above, 2nd figure.)
3. If a white sign falls to the side, it is the diminution of the good fortune indicated; if a black sign falls to the side, it is the diminution of the misfortune.

But Philippe May does not make the distinction of the character of the signs according to the fingers influenced. Our readers will only have to refer to the planets acting on each finger to fill this gap and to know the type of misfortune or blessing indicated by a sign.

6. THE MODIFYING SIGNS

Aside from the signs and mounds, there exist certain signs which *modify* the general indications for good or bad. Here are all the details necessary to understand concerning these signs.

a) The cross (See Fig. 41)

At the start of a line it impedes the character of this line. It is therefore:

- A bad sign if the line is good.

- A good sign if the line is bad.

At the end of a line it indicates the religious influence.

In the middle of a line it indicates a passing obstacle whose character is indicated by the significance of the line.

Alone upon the mound, it is always the sign of a good influence, of a raise, of an unexpected change in position.

b) The star

Same significance as the cross, but more intense. Indicates above all a fatal and unexpected event.

c) The square

Always a sign of preservation.

d) The point and ring.

Always a bad sign, especially if they are deep and colored. Destruction suffered by the good effects of the line in which they are encountered. Generally it is a nervous disease or an accident.

e) The isle

Ubiquity in the line where the isle is encountered. In the heart line, this will be the splitting of the affection, two friendships who are rivals at the same time; on the Mound of Venus, the dividing of legitimate or adulterous love; in the head line, the simultaneous splitting of the reasoning or the polarization of the reason, dangerous impulsive actions by excess reflection.

On the Study of lines or Chiromancy

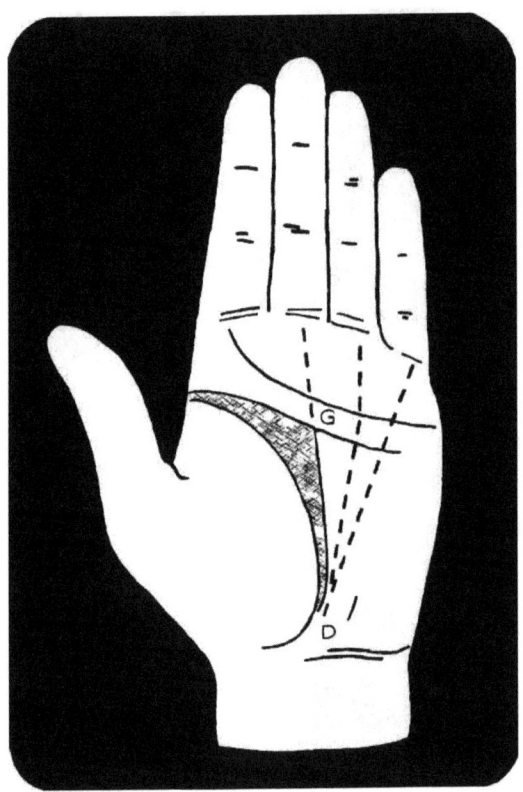

Figure 36
The Major Triangle

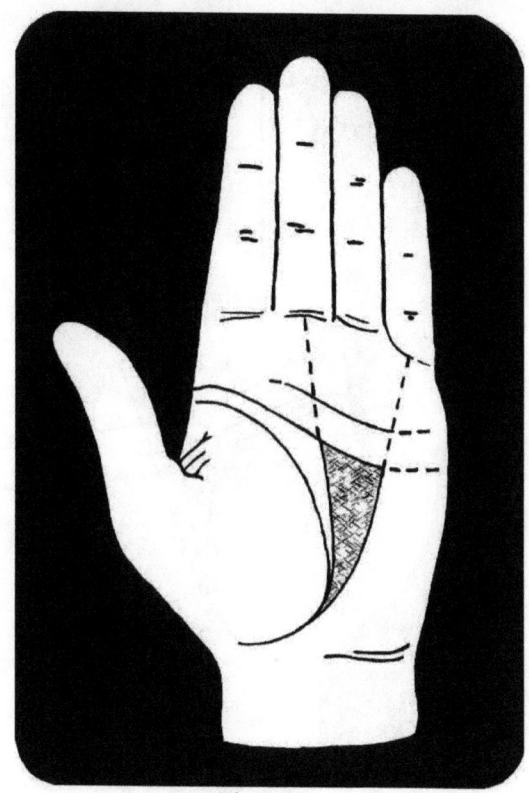

Figure 38
The Minor Triangle

On the Study of lines or Chiromancy

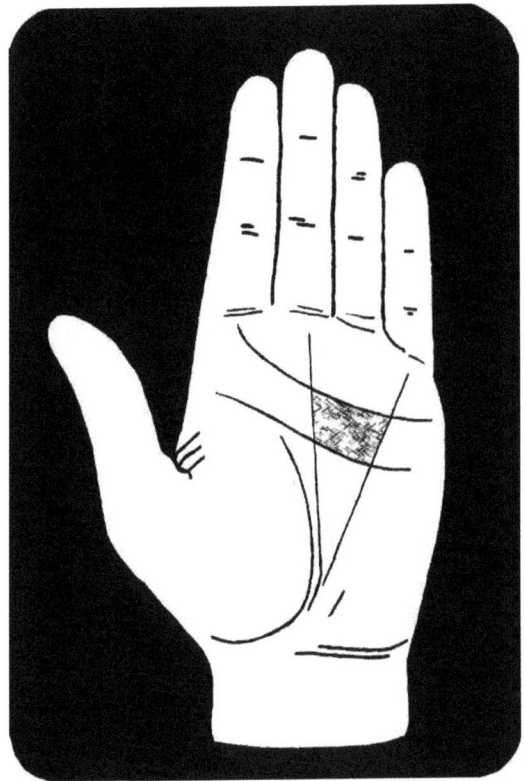

Figure 39
The Quadrangle

The Branches: Increases the strength of the lines and exaggerates the qualities or defects according to the type of line.

Double lines: Always amplify the influences of the mother-line.

Grills: Sign of excess in the significations of a mound or a line. On the Mound of Venus, it is perversity in love.

f) The triangle

Sign of providential influence. Indicates the aptitude to the mysterious sciences or the high protection of the invisible world according to the point where the triangle is found.

On the subject of these signs, we cannot counsel the curious reader too much to read the experimental facts enumerated by Desbarolles in the first part of his *Révélations complètes*.[8]

CHAPTER VI
Astrological Chiromancy

We have seen that chiromancy is attached, thanks to the astrological notions, to the different divinatory arts taught in the sanctuaries of Egypt.

Thus, certain individuals present certain hieroglyphs, beyond the sign of which we have just spoken, that the educated chiromancer must come to know well.

We give opposite a table of these signs, and we will furnish more in this section of the traditional astrological correspondences which are indispensible to every enthusiast desirous of perfecting himself in this art.

1. ASTROLOGICAL CORRESPONDENCES

a) Saturn

- *Indicates*: Fortune and misfortune, the melancholy things and affliction.

- *Is in itself*: Malign and major misfortune.

How to Read Hands

Figure 40
Signatures of the Planets in the hands
From top to bottom: Jupiter, Saturn, Sun,
Mercury, Moon, Mars, Venus

- *Some correspondences*: monks, hermits, curriers, cobblers, potters, all the melancholy arts. Laborers, misers. All the sordid works and offices.
- *Constitution*: Dry and cold with excess.

- *Colors that it gives to the hand*: Black, dark green, leaden hue.
- *Temperaments*: Pure melancholy (nervous). Melancholy mixed with sanguine (nerv. sanguine). Phlagmatic mixed with melancholy.
- *Signs*: Capricorn, Aquarius, Scorpio.
- *Elements*: Earth, earth mixed with air, earth mixed with fire.

b) Jupiter[9]

- *Indicates*: Honors, dignities, lesions and head wounds.
- *Is in itself*: Benign and major fortune.
- *Some correspondences*: Princes, ecclesiastics, priests, jurisconsults, senators, cardinals. Wealth. Laws. Profit. Politics and glory.
- *Constitution*: Hot and humid with moderation.
- *Color*: Red.
- *Temperament*: Choleric mixed with sanguine.
- *Sign*: Sagittarius.
- *Element*: Fire mixed with air.

c) Mars

- *Indicates*: Strength, anger, and the things which pertain to war.
- *Is in itself*: Malign and minor misfortune.
- *Some correspondences*: Surgeons, physicians, soldiers, lock-smiths, marshals. The audacious, the seditious, thieves, tyrants. All the cholerics. The great achievements. Metal-working. Chemistry.
- *Constitution*: Hot and dry to the utmost degree.
- *Color*: Color of fire.
- *Temperament*: Pure choleric.
- *Sign*: Aries.

- *Element*: Fire.

d) The Sun or Apollo

- *Indicates*: Friendships and enmities.

- *Is in itself*: Gentle, beneficent, and fortunate.

- *Some correspondences*: Barons, Princes, Marquis, magistrates. Noble and elevated spirits, the ambitious, gold, magnanimity, honor, splendor.

- *Constitution*: Moderately hot and dry.

- *Color*: Golden.

- *Temperament*: Yellow bile mixed with blood.

- *Sign*: Leo.

- *Element*: Fire mixed with air.

e) Venus

- *Indicates*: Lasciviousness or chastity, marriage or celibacy.

- *Is in itself*: Beneficent and minor fortune.

- *Some correspondences*: Singers, players of instruments, poets, tumblers, "flighty" women, painters, cooks. Sanguine men, love, humanity, music, luxury, lasciviousness, and other voluptuous things.

- *Constitution*: Extremely humid and less hot.

- *Colors*: Blue, citron color, pale green.

- *Temperament*: Pure sanguine. Sanguine mixed with phlegmatic.

- *Signs*: Libra, Taurus, Pisces.

- *Elements*: Air, air mixed with water.

f) Mercury

- *Indicates*: Judgment or stupidity. Ease or difficulty of speech.

- *Is in itself*: Indifferent. By itself, neither good nor bad.

- *Some correspondences*: Mathematicians, philosophers,

writers, minters, printers, booksellers, rhetoricians, merchants, sculptors, travels, invention, and novelties.

- *Constitution*: Moderately cold and humid.

- *Colors*: Ashy, color of iron.

- *Temperament*: Phlegmatic mixed with black bile. Black bile mixed with choleric.

- *Signs*: Gemini, Virgo.

- *Elements*: Water mixed with earth. Earth mixed with fire.

g) The Moon

- Indicates: Pilgrimages and travels, as much by sea as by earth.

- *Is in itself*: Somewhat fortunate and favorable.

- *Some correspondences*: Hunters, fishers, curriers, coachmen, sailors (all those of the river and the sea), humid illnesses and infirmities.

- *Constitution*: Excessively cold and humid.

- *Color*: White.

- *Temperament*: Pure phlegmatic.

- *Sign*: Cancer.

- *Element*: Water

2. INTERPRETATION OF THE SIGNS

While the ignorant who has come to know vaguely some signs, recites his lesson without intelligence, the true chiromancer must discover, by reasoning, the significance of a sign new for him.

To that end, it is above all necessary to learn to use well two indispensible processes:

1. The exact determination of the signs.
2. The interpretation of the signs.

It is especially upon the interpretation that we must

insist in order to make of our readers true artists and not parrots. This will allow them to discover by themselves a multitude of ideas whose collection rends obscure and incomprehensible the majority of the classical treatises on chiromancy.

The interpretation includes several parts that we are going to deconstruct to the best of our ability.

1. Strictly exact establishment of the astrological correspondences.

2. Translation of the astrological hieroglyphs and their signification in common language.

3. Synthesis of all these facts determined by this translation. Determination of the ages. Some examples are going to clarify these notions.

a) Establishment of the astrological correspondences

Let us consider Figure 41 which presents four signs: A, B, C, D, that we are to study carefully.

Let us begin by naming them astrologically:

A. - Line of mars or head line is inclined towards the end or upon the Mound of the Moon, and forms a cross.

B. - A cross is found on the heart line or line of Jupiter under the Mound of Apollo, which is streaked by three small vertical lines.

C. - Three lines depart from the end of the life line (Venusian); the first of these lines come to join the Mercurian; the second is terminated abruptly; and the third is terminated by a cross.

Astrological Chiromancy

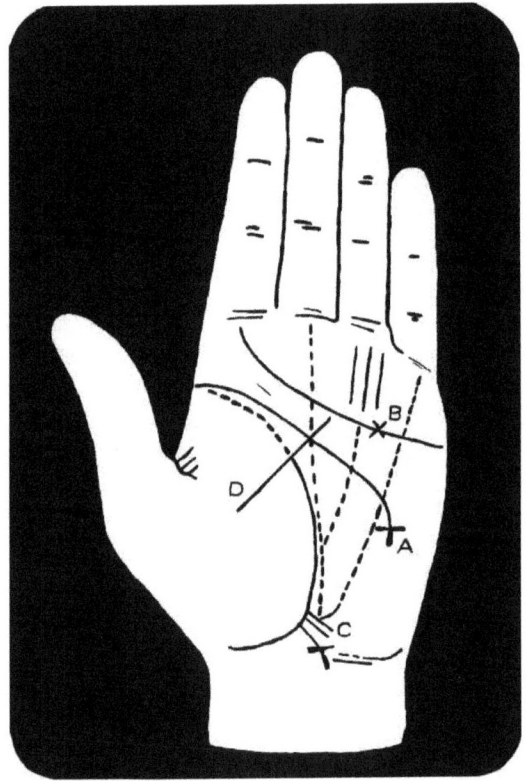

Figure 41
Astrological Correspondences

D. - A line cuts the life line, meets the Saturnian and the head line at their crossing, and comes to be closed abruptly on the heart line.

These are four examples which will serve as models for all the other cases.

b) Translation of the astrological hieroglyphs in symbols.

A. - The head line is inclined towards the Mound of the Moon and forms a cross.

- *Head line*: Essentially masculine in all that relates to the spirit and to reasoning.

- *Mound of the Moon*: Imagination, dreams, mysticism.

- *The cross*: Near the Mound of the Moon indicates the religious character of mysticism.

TRANSLATION OF THIS SIGN: Reason will lead you to faith, and you will go on to understand the mysticism.

B. - *Cross in the middle of a line*: Obstacles.

- *Heart line*: Essentially feminine; the heart, passion.

- *Mound of Apollo*: Art, fortune, or glory.

TRANSLATION OF THIS SIGN: An obstacle of sentimental origin which influences art or the artistic career.

C. - According to Madam Marie Burlen (l'Arc-en-ciel) these lines indicate children. The first will be a merchant or physician (line of Hermes or Mercury). The second will die, and the third will be religious (cross at the end).

D. - *The life line cut*: profound modification to existence.

Crossing the plain of Mars and cutting the head line: Importance of the will in this modification. This modification is personal and it does not come from the outside.

Ending of the heart line: This modification tended towards the fusion of the life with the heart.

TRANSLATION: Impulsive act because of an affair of the heart.

c) Synthesis and general laws - Determination of the ages

The readers, familiar with the teachings of the classical

treatises on chiromancy, will pause at the translations that we have given above.

These translations are not complete, for they lack therein the precision of time in which these various events have occurred, and the means to know whether these events pertain to the past or to the future.

Desbarolles, who remains the uncontested master of modern chiromancy, gives a great deal on the divisions of the life line; but he does not give the divisions by age of any other line. We believe to have been one of the first, if not the first, among the contemporaries, to study the Saturnian from this point of view, and the practice has allowed us to assert the value of our divisions. By the *head line* and the *heart line*, we will modify our divisions by adopting those of Philippe May de Franconie until experimental verification.

It is in relying on these notions that one will complete the translations that we have given.

A. - The modification or course of the head line being found under the diminished perpendicular of the area of the Mound of Apollo, *the event indicated will occur at the age of 50*.

B. - The cross being found under the heart line and in the area of the Mound of Apollo, *the event will occur at the age of 20*.

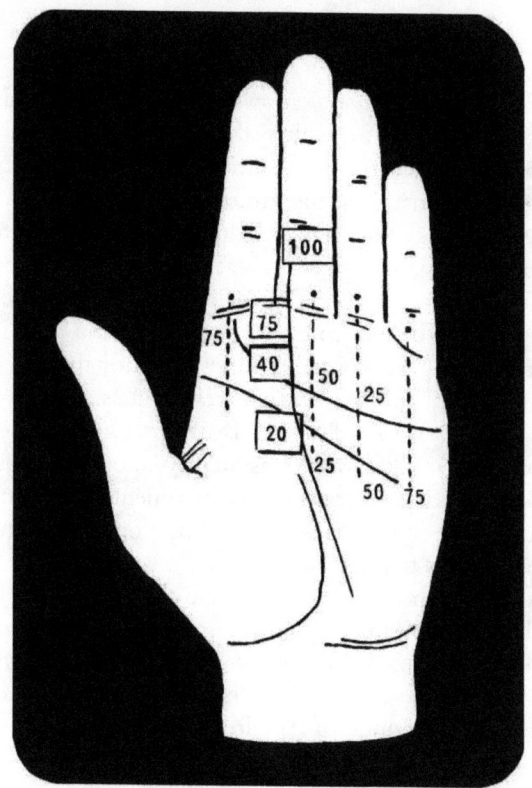

Figure 42
The ages of the lines for the determinations of the duration of life.

Astrological Chiromancy

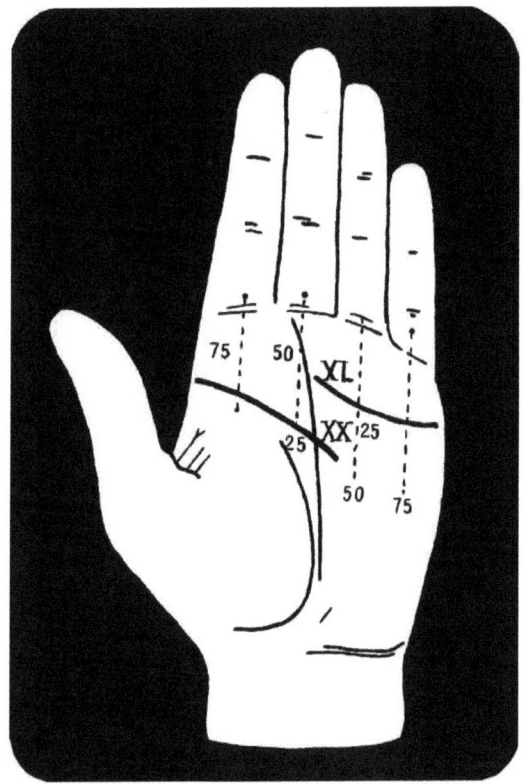

Figure 43
Death at about 45 years old.

ASTROLOGICAL RELATIONS OF ASPECTS

The practitioners who wish to push the precision even further would take into account all the influences exercised immediately or indirectly by the planets bordering upon each sign.

3. HOW TO DETERMINE, EVEN APPROXIMATELY, THE DURATION OF LIFE

The majority of authors refer to this subject, according to tradition, by the length of the line of Venus or *life line*. The experience, that I have pursued personally for eleven years, permits us to assert that these indications are *absolutely false*, and that there exists no connection between the age of death and the length of the life line. This line seems to indicate *the age of the characteristic* rather than the duration of existence. Thus, a young man of 20 years, dead at 21 of consumption, had a life line surrounding the Mound of Venus, which indicated 70 or 80 years of existence. But this young man had always been remarkable by his precocity and the seriousness of his character.

For a long time we have believed, that there did not exist any chiromantic sign on this point, and yet certain exact predictions of bohemians induced us to not abandon our research into this subject. For some months we have pursued a new path that we are eager to point out to the seekers, in order to group upon this question the most experiments possible.

The determination of the duration of life can only be the result of a *mean* that we advise to establish in the following manner. (System of May perfected.) (See Fig. 44.)

a) Sign of the head

Three perpendiculars dropped successively, from the middle of the finger of Saturn, from the middle of the finger of Apollo, and from the middle of the finger of Mercury upon the head line, gives respectively 25, 50, and 75 years.

Astrological Chiromancy

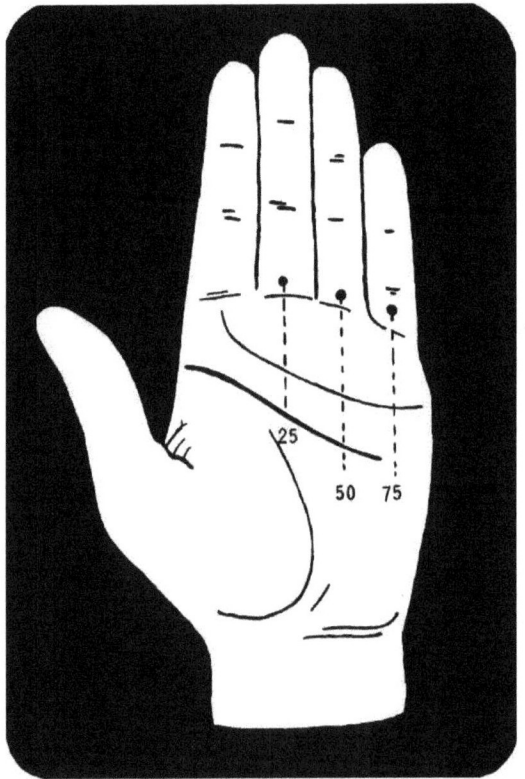

Figure 44
The ages of the head line

We begin, then, by determining the age given by the length of the head line.

Let us suppose that the line gives 70 years.

b) Sign of the heart

The same perpendiculars, increase by another departing from the middle of the index (finger of Jupiter) and leaving aside that of the finger of Mercury, gives respectively 25, 60, and 75 years. Let us suppose that this line give 60 years in the hand taken as example.

c) Sign of Saturn

The Saturnian cuts the line of the head at 20 years, the line of the heart at 40 years, and the first phalanx of the finger of Saturn at 75 years.

Let us suppose that the Saturnian indicates 65 years in the hand taken as example.

d) Establishing the mean.

One writes, under one another, the ages indicated by the three lines, that is to say:

$$\begin{array}{r} 70 \\ 60 \\ \underline{65} \\ 195 \end{array}$$

and we perform addition. We then divide the result obtained by three (the number of lines) and we obtain the mean of the age corresponding to the end of life, that is to say in the example that we have chosen:

$$\frac{195}{3} = 65 \text{ years}$$

It goes without saying that one may establish this mean by taking into account the life line and the line of Mercury if one believes to have, thanks to these lines, sincere indications.

4. HOW THE HAND IS TO BE READ.

1. Chirognomy of the wrist, of the palm (the

mounds), of the fingers and the nails, of the thumb; in order to establish the impulses of the passions and the character.

2. Chiromancy of the wrist in order to pose the first deductions on the health.

3. Chiromancy of the palm by taking up the mounds again and in studying successively:

A. - The connections of the lines of life, the head, the heart, and the Saturnian in order to accentuate the details concerning the character.

B. - Detailed study of each line in the following order:
- Head line.
- Life line.
- Heart line and ring of Venus.
- Line of Apollo, Mercury, and the Moon (if it is there).

Finally, end with the Saturnian, which indicates the age of the principal events.

C. - This is indispensible, to determine the duration of life by the mean of the lines of the heart, head, and Saturn.

4. Chiromancy of the fingers

Take up again the study of the nails, of the phalanxes, and study the signs which are on each phalanx. Determine the approaching events, according to the marks of the nails.

5. - CONCLUSION OF CHIROMANCY

If the chirognomy has furnished us the means to specify the character and the impulses of the passions, we see how chiromancy is rich in details concerning the events and their determination. It remains to us now, to end our work, to enter upon the most abstract part of our study: the research of the causes, or the chirosophy which forms the truly philosophical section of this art.

Figure 45
Symbolic image of the hand by Desbarolles

THIRD PART
CHIROSOPHY

CHAPTER VII
Chirosophy or study of the causes

Chirosophy has for its object of study the *principles* of the art which occupies us. Being elevated above facts and even laws, chirosophy strives to determine the raison d'être of the shapes and lines previously analyzed. It is in this way that it allows one to grasp the bonds which attach chiromancy to the other sciences of divination. No classical author has, up to the present, dedicated a special study to this section, and yet, a volume would be necessary in order to treat this subject completely. But as this study is above all attached to the general philosophy, we will give here only a short summary intended to fix the principal points that others than us will surely perfect later on.

1. THE CHIROSOPHY OF THE SHAPES AND THE ASTRAL BODY

The first question that is necessary for us to resolve is that of knowing what is the raison d'être *of the shapes* of the human being. We will thus determine the philosophy of chirognomy, or the chirognomic chirosophy.

The celebrated experiments of the physiologist Flourens have proven that all the cells which constitute the material part of our being (our corpse, to call it by its true name) die and are replaced in a time that one may estimate at seven years, bones included. When we see a person seven years after our first encounter, *none of the material cells which existed then still exist*; the physical body has entirely transformed, and yet, it has not lost its form. We easily recognize the forms already seen seven years ago.

This indicates to us that the physical body is the product of *something* which fabricates its material elements and which gives them their *form*. This something acts outside of our consciousness, and acts still even when we sleep, since our lungs and our stomach function and our arteries beat during sleep. The physiologists have indeed determined *how* this something acts; they will tell us that it is thanks to the great sympathetic nerve and its multiple ganglions that the arteries beat, that the lymphatics function, and that the organic exchanges, as well as the proper placement of the new cells and the elimination of the used cells, is accomplished. But this nerve is like a telegraphic wire, its ganglions are like the telegraphic apparatus which are simply *tools* permitting the telegraphist to handle the electricity, and the "something" of which we have spoken to handle the nervous force.

It is indeed thanks to the ganglions of the grand sympathetic that this "something" acts to create the forms of the organism, and a daily experiment is going to show it to us.

If you cut your finger slightly, what happens to it? The "something" of which we do not yet know the name, is going to repair your finger without you having to occupy yourself with it; and this repair will be so perfect that the finest of little lines of your finger will be remade in its slightest details (which proves, by the way, the action of the nerve centers on the formation of the lines). That is what happens if the cut is slight and only breaks the skin and the superficial muscles.

But what if the cut is deep and it goes to the periosteum? Then a greater repair is necessary. In its

Chirosophy or study of the causes

integrity, it will have a scar. *Do we ask why?*

Why, the physiologist will tell us, because you have touched the ganglion (or ganglions) of the grand sympathetic attached to the periosteum. It is how if you destroy the telegraphic apparatus of the desk receiver, the communication cannot be transmitted.

This "something" has indeed wished to remake the tissues in their first form, but it no longer has a center of indispensible drainage, and must be content with any reparation whatever.

All this shows us that the forms of our physical body are the result of the action of this "something" that we must now try to name.

The physiologists call it *Organic Life*. But this name suits better the nervous force which travels through the filaments of the grand sympathetic, rather than the principle which sets this force into motion. The Organic Life is the electricity of the telegraph, *it is not the telegraphist*. Let us look for another name.

The psychologists will call it the *unconscious*, and they will already be closer to the truth; for they will indicate by this name the independence of this "something" vis-à-vis our consciousness, and they will differentiate by this that something of our self-consciousness, made capital from the philosophical point of view. But the term *Unconscious* does not convey this capital property, this physiological action that we have just analyzed.

According to what we have said, the physical body is no more than a material stretched over another thing which gives it form. The physical body is an inert glove which borrows its form from the living hand that it contains. We may therefore already call this "something" the *formative body*, and we thus have a name clearly expressing the functions of this principle. Now it is necessary for us to return to the *tradition*.

The Hermetic philosophers, to whom we owe the first creation, since the middle ages, of all these sciences of which we are so proud, possessed their philosophical principles from the ancient Egyptian sanctuaries. Thus, they took great care not to separate the metaphysical from the physical, and they had even pushed the love of abstraction a little further. Since then, astrology has given way to astronomy, alchemy to chemistry, and magic to physics.

Thus an enormous reaction was produced, and for two centuries they cultivated only astronomy, chemistry, and physics, while considering the metaphysical part of these sciences, that is to say astrology, alchemy, and magic, as hazy absurdities. However, in our day, certain seekers have had the idea to return to the study of these occult sciences and a new reaction manifests itself, tending to render justice to these philosophers, for the most part so misunderstood. We study the conception that they had of man, and discover in their works long chapters dedicated to this formative body of which we have spoken. But instead of calling it the *formative body*, they consider it as acting in man as the stars act (according to astrology) in the Universe, and they call it the "ASTRAL BODY."

Through respect for the tradition, just as we have preserved the name of Chiromancy, we preserve the name of ASTRAL BODY in order to indicate this *unconscious principle which gives form to our organs, which rebuilds as much as possible the destroyed forms, and which presides over all the organic exchanges which maintain life in the human organism.*

But, to constitute the forms, does this ASTRAL BODY

make use of types all different from one another, or does it act by starting from a *general* form which it modifies more or less according to the circumstance? According to the teachings of the Hermetic tradition, confirmed by the recent study of homologic repetitions, it is necessary to respond affirmatively to this question: yes, all the forms of the human being are slight modifications of a general type that one finds repeated everywhere.

And as this general type is immediately modified by the intimate character of the spirit of man, of his immortal principle, we see how the indications of this modification, *repeated in all the details of the organic forms*, will allow us to ascend from the study of these forms, to the origin of their modification, and to find again everywhere the intimate character of the human being which has everywhere imprinted its "signature." - From here comes the sciences of divination.

If one studies the modifications of the general type produced in the shape of the cranium, we will find again the modifying character, thanks to the indications of PHRENOLOGY.

And if we address ourselves to the modifications produced in the shapes of the face? It is PHYSIOGNOMY which will respond.

But what if one holds to the modifications produced in the limbs? In the hands? It is CHIROGNOMY which informs us.

From here, there are two important conditions: first: the raison d'être of the sciences of divination, then the narrow connection which unites all these sciences to one another.

Thus, the PHYSICAL BODY is fabricated by the

ASTRAL BODY, and the ASTRAL BODY may be influenced immediately by the SPIRIT, which permits the destruction of the impulses that the SPIRIT sustains from the forms given to the PHYSICAL BODY by the ASTRAL BODY, or the reactions that the ASTRAL BODY sustains on the part of the SPIRIT from the hieroglyphic signs and lines inscribed on the brow or the hands. - Such are the foundations of CHIROSOPHY.

We see the importance that occultism attaches to this "ASTRAL BODY." We must not believe that it is a question here solely of an hypothesis, and we have seen in these last years a conscientious scholar arrive at the experimental demonstration of this astral body. The readers, that this interests, may refer to the work of M. the lieutenant-colonel de Rochas: *"L'Extériorisation de la Sensibilité."*

2. CHIROSOPHY OF THE LINES AND SIGNS. WHY ARE THERE LINES IN THE HAND?

a) The hand is the face of the astral body. Do the lines become modified?

The notions concerning this question are related to the most technical teachings of the Occult Science. The reader, little familiarized with these teachings, ought not, then, be frightened of the apparent obscurity of some of the lines below, written specially for the students already advanced.

Man is the summarized microcosm of the Universe. Man ought, then, to reflect in his constitution the three planes: MATERIAL, ASTRAL, and DIVINE, which constitute the microcosm. It is indeed that which is produced by the constitution of man in three centers: material or abdominal, vital or thoracic, and psychic or cephalic. Each of these centers is, besides, itself hierarchized into three parts, as has determined Malfalti de Montereggio in his "*Mathèse*."

Each of these centers corresponds to one of the planes of the Universe:

- the abdominal center corresponds to the material plane;

- the thoracic center answers to the astral plane;

- and the cephalic center to the divine plane. Moreover, the face synthesizes in it the influences of the three planes.
- Each of the human centers has a pair of members charged with manifesting in nature the influence of this center.

To the abdomen are attached the abdominal members, to the chest the thoracic members, and to the head the cephalic members (jaw-bone and larynx). It is in the shape and in the exterior manifestations of these members that we see the character of each of the centers of the human being.

The instinctive impulses will therefore be revealed by the study of the gait; the vital or sentimental impulses by the study of the gestures; and the psychic impulses, by the study of the word. The gaze will synthesize all the impulses. This is the key of all the sciences of divination.

Now, chiromancy, which interests us here, is concerned with the hand, that is to say with the organ of expression corresponding to the vital center of man, domain of the grand sympathetic nerve, and to the astral world in the Universe, domain of the formative forces. *The hand is therefore the face of organic life*, as the countenance is the face of conscious life. Thus, all the astral *impulses* that the organic life is charged to execute within us by means of the grand sympathetic nerve, are marked in the hand. That is why there are lines in the hand. That is also why experiment shows that *to the degree which the will acts further upon the unconscious impulses, the lines are modified*, which proves again the absolute integrity of the human will. That is also why the affections which modify the organic life and the grand sympathetic nerve profoundly, also act upon the lines of the hand which may disappear more or less completely under such an influence. That is also why experiment has shown us that twenty-four hours after death, the lines of the hand disappear, beginning with the small lines.

Such is the solution of some important questions that our personal studies, for nearly ten years, have allowed us to resolve as best we can.

b) Why we are sometimes deceived. Importance of the will.

The chiromantic signs indicate the impulses to which the person is subjected whose hand is examined; but these signs cannot specify the changes which will be brought about by the will into these impulses. This is a justification of the old Hermetic adage: *Astra inclinant, non necessitant*.

When we have dealings with an extremely willful nature, it can happen then that all these deductions fall untrue, since you relate the *impulses* that the will of the individual delights in breaking in proportion to their appearance.

Have, therefore, ever present to the mind, the history of Socrates who, accused by a physiognomist of having all the vices, replied to his disciples who protested: "This man has reason; I have an *inclination of the passions* towards all the vices, which the diviner sees in my traits. But my will has broken these impulses, which the divine cannot see." The power of the will is such that it can modify the signs, which then become what they really are: *warnings*.

c) Providence warns us through the signs

Human liberty is so entire that no power may impair it.

Providence, to which every man who aspires to regeneration ought to join forces, can only warn us of the dangers which threaten us, without having the faculty to compel our will to avoid these dangers.

We are similar, in life, to a man walking at night upon a road full of moats and precipices. Providence cannot, if we call it to our aid, fill these moats, hollowed out by our previous faults, or raise us from the earth in order to cross them. Its power is limited to lighting our path, thus leaving full liberty to our will; for if we close our eyes, or if we put on a blindfold, we fall into the precipices that its light had permitted us to avoid.

So the *signs* of providential action shine numerous and varied around us; they are written in letters of fire in the air, then upon all the beings of nature, and inscribed in universal characters in our traits and in our hands. But foolish vanity puts a blindfold over our eyes, and we say: "There is no Providence," while it would suffice to open our eyes in order to see and bless its efforts, unceasingly in our favor.

3. CHIROSOPHY OF THE HAND IN GENERAL

The general type that the astral body reproduces in the details of the organism is manifested by the triple division of the human being in abdomen, chest, and head, with the members attached to each of these sections. Each of the members reproduces its triple division: thigh, leg, foot, arm, forearm, hand, the general type of which is found again in the subdivisions: ankle, foot, toes, and wrist, palm, fingers. Each finger reproduces the law again by its triple constitution in phalanx, middle phalanx, and ungual phalanx.

If, then, we recall that all the identical segments correspond, we say:
1. Abdomen, thigh, arm, wrist, phalanx.
2. Chest, leg, forearm, palm, middle phalanx.
3. Head, foot, hand, fingers, ungual phalanx.

That is to say that all the forms of the organs of the first line allow one to determine the *instincts*, corresponding to the material world.

All the forms of the organs of the second line allow one to determine the sentiments, corresponding to the astral world.

And all the forms of the organs of the third line allow one to determine the *ideas*, corresponding to the divine world.

Everything will depend, therefore, on the *point of view* from which one will be placed, since *ungual phalanx* would suffice in a strict sense to indicate the teachings inscribed in the entire hand. But leaving for the moment these correspondences, we must keep ourselves to the study of the hand considered in its triple constitution, in wrist, palm, and fingers. Let us look, therefore, at what this hand is.

Considered philosophically, the hand is the organ of gesture. But there are two organs of gesture, a right and a left, serving each of the two halves of the human being; the right half and the left[10] half, or to say better, each hand is half of the organ of gesture of which one obtains the complete figure only in reuniting the two hands as shows the adjoining figure. It is from here that we are going to be able to draw our deductions.

Chirosophy or study of the causes

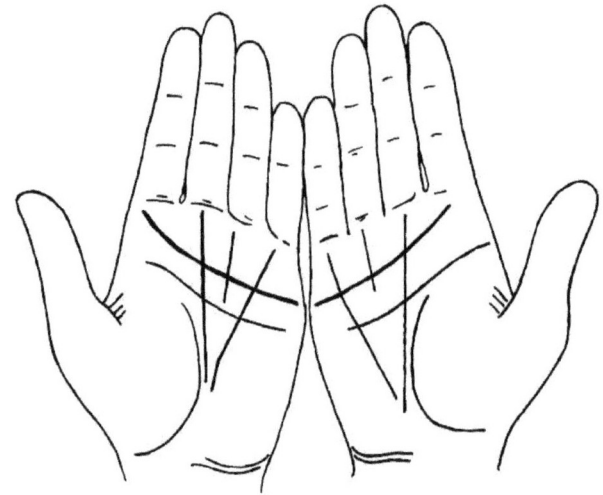

Figure 46
The organ of the complete Gesture
Note: the continuity of the two heart lines.

The simple organs, that is to say manifested by a sole exemplar, like the nose, the mouth, etc., are formed by the union of the two symmetrical halves, and the double organs like the eyes, the ears, the arms, or the hands, are formed by the individual existence of each of the symmetrical halves. The hemiplegia proves this by paralyzing *one* eyelid, *one* arm, *one* hand, and *half* of the mouth or *half* of the nose (as regards its folds).

One hand, therefore, corresponds to *one half* of the body: the wrist corresponds to one half of the abdomen, the palm to one half of the chest, and the fingers to one half of the head. The thumb corresponds to one arm and the Mound of Venus to the shoulder.

This is what Figure 47 shows us.

If we place ourselves at the point of view of the analogous comparison of the entire hand with the half of the body, we see how the teachings of the tradition are found justified.

a) The palm

The palm of the hand may be considered as a semi-chest ruling the abdomen- wrist upon which comes to be grouped at the top the head, fingers, and on the side the arm, thumb. Anatomical considerations, which would be misplaced, would show this again here. We may therefore consider this figure as sufficiently clear for us to avoid developing what connections the wrist and palm have, and we are going to remain a little on the fingers.

b) The fingers

The fingers require a special study, because they alone constitute a complete analogical organ with its three divisions, phalanx, middle phalanx, ungual phalanx.

If we relate it to the figure formed by the two hands united into one, we see that the two little fingers juxtaposed may be considered as a single organ and that then the complete organ of gesture is formed of *seven fingers* and two thumbs.

Chirosophy or study of the causes

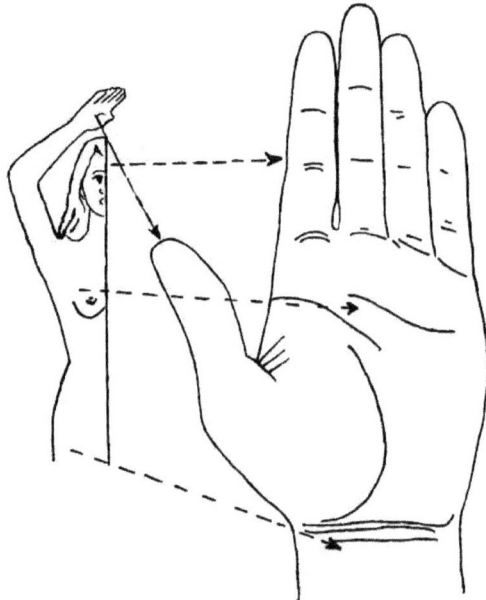

Figure 47
The Hand and Body Correspondences

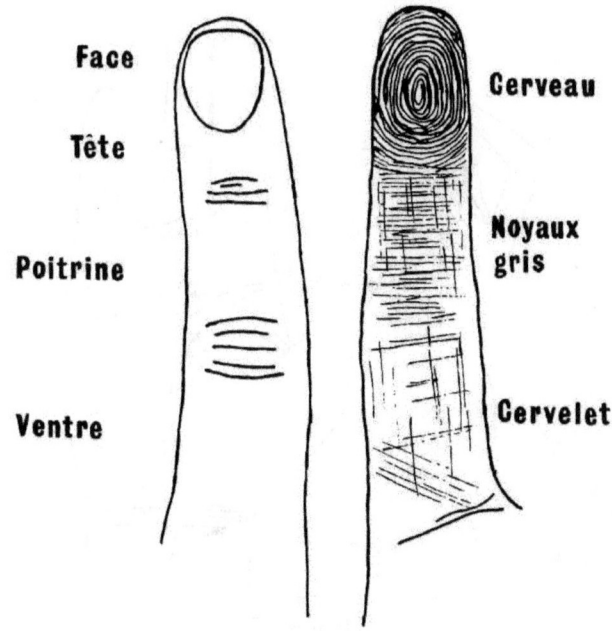

Figure 48
The fingers

Left side, top to bottom: Face, Head, Chest, Abdomen
Right side: Brain, Grey cells, Cerebellum

Each finger is to be considered under its two faces, the nailed face and the palmar face. The nailed side corresponds to the visible, exterior part of the individual, to the physical body and its forms (this is the only usefulness in chirognomy); and the palmar side to the invisible, inner part of the individual, to the nerve centers, and to the astral body.

Thus, to the nail, which is in some sort the face of the finger, is opposed to the palmar portion of the ungual phalanx covered by ellipsoidal lines, images of the cerebral circumvolutions.[11]

In this case the middle phalanx corresponds to the grey cells and the phalanx to the cerebellum, which would be related to the three correspondences of the phalanxes: idea, action, and instinct.

It is indeed curious to note that the cerebral substance is situated in the cranium in three layers. The superior layer in front contains the circumvolutions which preside, above all, over ideation. The middle layer contains the other circumvolutions as well as the principal grey cells. And the inferior layer is reserved nearly exclusively to the cerebellum. One may thus understand the correspondences or the division of the fingers.

Each of the fingers indicates, therefore, a particular cerebral impulse corresponding to a single localization, and this indication is realized under two aspects: actively (predominance of action) in the right hand; passively (predominance of idea) in the left hand. Until more amply informed, the astrological correspondences may suffice to characterize these impulses.

4. COMPARATIVE CHIROMANCY

It is to this section that is attached comparative chiromancy.

Comparative chiromancy has for its aim, being given a line or shape of the hand, to deduce therefrom the form of writing or the forms of the face of the consultant, and to determine the writing and physiognomy of its complementary.

This work demands to it alone long developments,

which we will give in our *Traité de divination déductive* currently in preparation.

Our readers, that these studies would interest, may while waiting, consult the little work of *Chiromancie et de Ceraphologie comparée* by Mr. Louis Mond, who has had the intuition of this part of chiromancy.

We have likewise given the elements of this study in *les Arts divinatoires*, a small brochure formed from our studies published in the journal *Le Figaro*.

CHAPTER VIII
Little dictionary of chiromancy

We have thought it useful to place at the end of our work a small dictionary giving the preincipal chiromantic indications concerning the current life. This is a simple essay that we will develop later. The abbreviations indicate:

BUR. *Marie Burlen.* "L 'arc-en-Ciel. "
DEB. *Desbarolles.* "*Mystères de la Main. Révélations complètes.*"
TRAD. Tradition.

Adultery. - Isle on the Mound of Venus emitting a line which cuts the life line (Deb.).

Avarice. - Long and straight head line (Deb.).

Children. - Vertical lines at the end of the life line and going towards the rascette (Bur.).

Condemnation to Death or Forced Labor. - The life, head, and heart lines are united under Saturn (Trad.).

Crime. - Deep, black points.
1. Upon the life line.
2. Upon the lines relating to the genre of crime (Trad.).

Lines cut and deformed at the rascette.

Devotion. - Small crosses at the top of the non-nailed phalanx of the thumb (Bur.).

Family. - The lines which start out from the Mound of Venus while cutting the life line, before the age of the love indicates the family and its influences (Deb.).

Fatal Love. - A line starting out from the Mound of Venus, cuts the life line and all the lines in order to come to an end at the mound which rules the person that one has loved (Deb.).

Fortune. - Very large line of Apollo (Deb.).

Gambling, Gaming. - Finger of the Sun as long as the finger of Saturn (Deb.)

Illness. - Meeting of the heart line and life line with small head line. The planetary signature of the consultant indicates the type of illness (Deb.).

Inheritance. - Cross in the middle of the rascette. As many crosses, that many inheritances (Trad.).

Inheritance. - Small line parallel to the life line, starting from the fold of flexion of the thumb (Bur.).

Lawsuit. - Transversal line starting from the Mound of Venus, cutting the life line to come to a stop on the Saturnian where it ends in a star. The life line indicates the age of the lawsuit (Deb.).

Legacy. - A square at the superior part of the Mound of Venus under Jupiter (Bur.).

Lover (Abandonment of). - Star on the line of Apollo. This star is tied to the line which indicates the age of the event (Deb.).

Marriage. - Large horizontal line between the root of the little finger and the heart line, at the percussion (Trad.).

Mediumistic Abilities. - A line of the Moon at Mercury. The head line descends towards the Moon. Mound of the Moon streaked (Deb.).

Passing Union. - Little signs placed at the horizontal percussion after the Mound of Mercury.

Politics (Great Success). - Grill on the Mound of Jupiter (Bur.).

Preservation. - A square regarding a deadly sign always preserves from the influences of this sign (Trad.).

Rich Marriage Despite Poverty. - A long triangle on the rascettes (Bur.).

Sectary. - Religious persecution. Faculties grafted on the oblique line which cuts in two the first phalanx of the thumb (Bur.).

Travel by Sea. - Horizontal line or the Mound of the Moon (Trad.).

Union (Line of). - At the percussion between the heart line and the root of Mercury, horizontal.

BIBLIOGRAPHY

In order to put the studious readers in a position to pursue at their will the study of Chiromancy, we will see to follow our treaties with a bibliography as complete as possible.

Aristotle. - "*Cyromancia Aristotelis*" *cum figuris*. 1490. 1721 third.

Belot. - The works of Mr. Jean Belot, cure of Mal-Monti, professor of divine and celestial sciences, consisting of the "*Chiromancie, Physionomie,*" "*l'Art de memoire de Raymond Lulle*"; "*Traité des Divinations, Augures et Songes*"; "*les Sciences sténographique,*" Paulines, Armadelles et Lullistes; "*l'Art dedoctement prècher et haranguer*, etc." - Last edition, revised, corrected and enlarged with various treatises.

"*La Chiromancie Médicinale,*" followed by a treatise on physiognomy and another on the marks of the nails, by Philippe May de Franconie, translated from the German by P.H. Treusches, de Wezhauzen with a foreword and Synthetic Chiromancy by Ernest Bose. Paris.

Ernest Bose (see May, Philippe). - Mr. Bose has published in the journal "*Le Voile d'Isis,*" a "Bibliographie générale des Sciences occultes," from which we have borrowed some numbers relative to Chiromancy.

Marie Burlen. - "*L'Arc-en-ciel*." 1 beautiful volume in-18, decorated with figures. Paris, 1894.
Very good treatise, very personal and containing some excellent things.

Catan. - "Chiromancy."

Chifro's. - "*Language of the hand.*" New York, 1694. "*La Chirognomonie*" ou l'art de connaître les tendances de l'Intillymée, d'après les formes de la main, by Captain S. d'Arpentigny. - Paris, 1 vol. in-8vo, 1863.

1729. "*La Clef d'Or*" or the art of winning at the lottery, followed by a treatise on physiognomy and chiromancy by a modern cabalist, in-18, 34 illus. Lille, s.d.

1736. Cocles (B). - "*Le Compendium de physiognomonie et chiromancie.*" 1 vol. in-8vo. Paris, 1546.

1731. Colombière (de la). - "*Traité de la physiognomie.*" Vol. in-8vo. Paris, 1660.

1732. Corum (Adrien). - "*L'Art de la chiromancie.*" In-8vo, n.p.n.d. (around 1530?).

1733. Same. - "*Les Indéscretions de la main,*" original text translated from Latin into French by Jean de Verdelay. Small in-8vo with figures. Paris, 1878 - Reprint of the treatise on chiromancy from the 16th century. (Bibliography by E. Bose).

Marius Decrespe. - "*La Main et ses mystères.*" 2 vol. in-18 with fig. 1895. Well made work and useful to consult. Does not take into account some errors of detail.

Desbarolles. - "*Les Mystères de la Main révélés et expliqué,*" 1859.

Very good work become impossible to find and replaced advantageously by the following.

"*Mystères de la Main, révélations complètes,*" with 300 explanatory illustrations, 3rd edition. 1 vol. in-4to. Paris. The classic treatise on chiromancy, recommended
to our readers for the details.

1739. Desbarolles. - "Almanach de la Main." Years 1867, 1868, 1869, in-18.
Paris.

"*Petits mystères de la Destinée*" by Joseph Balsamo. 1 vol. in-18. Garnier brothers, publishers. (Around 1860). One of the rare treatises where we find something on the chiromancy of the fingers.

"*Die Kunst Ciromantia*," 1475. (Found in the British Museum.)

Dryandrus. - "*De Chiromantia*," bk. III. Malpurgie, 1538. The most ancient treatise known on chiromancy after the previous.

Geber (Jehan). - Very brief treatise on "*Chiromantique physionomie.*" In-8vo. Paris, Guillaume Noir. 1557. (Bibliogr. by E. Bose).

Grandpre (J. de). - "*L'Art de prédire l'avenir.*" Divination by the stars, the hand, writing, physiognomy, shape of the skull, the cards, numbers, dreams, visions, magnetism, somnambulism, spiritism, sorcery, crystography (for crystallagraphy), etc. Gr. in-8vo. Paris, n.d. - The author has wished to make a synthesis of the occult sciences, but he succeeds only in composing a sort of Japanese salad of compilations as little interesting as it is incoherent. (E. Bose.)

Halbert (d'Angers). - "*La Cartomancie*" enlarged with a course on chiromancy. Paris, in-12mo, n.d.

Good summary with the use of the fields.

1753. Indagine. - "*Chiromantia, Physiognomia, Astrologia naturalis,*" 1 vol. p. in-8vo with fig. on wood. Parisiis, P. Drouart, n.d. (Bibliogr. by Mr. E. Bose).

"*Le livre magique!*" History of supernatural events and personages including details on Demonology, Astrology, and Chiromancy, etc. Paris, in-18, Corbei the Elder, 1835.

Leclercq. - "*La Chiromancie et ce qu'il taut en croire.*" Encyclopedic Review of 15 March, 1895. - Pretentious article by a beginner which offers some value only by the reproductions of hands and the judgments of Mme de

Thèbes.

1759. May de Franconie (Philippe). - "*La Chiromancie Médicinale*," accompanied by a treatise on physiognomy and another on the marks which appear on the finger- nails; composed entirely in German and translated into French by Philippe-Henry de Wezhauzen, 1 small vol. in-12mo of 12 ff. and 136 pages, very rare work, at The Hague, with Levijunav Dyck, 1665; all copies are signed by the author. This work has been republished and enlarged by Mr. Ernest Bose.

Mond (Louis M.). - "*La Chiromancie et la Graphologie comparée.*" Little brochure in-18, circa 1887. First work where the study of comparative chiromancy is approached.

Papus. - "*Traité synthétique de Chiromancie.*" Broch. ill. in-8vo of 32 pp., 1892.

Peruchio (1633). - "*Chiromancie.*" Good work, the details are well treated.

Plytoff. - "*La Magie*," 1 vol. in-18, with Baillère (1893).

"*Mystères des Sciences Occultes*," by An Initiate (1893). These two works by Mr. Plytoff contain some notions on chiromancy. Also Almanach Hachette (1894), Chiromancy art. by the same author.

Ronphyle. - "*La Chiromancie naturelle.*" (Paris, Baptiste Loyson, 1665), in-8vo. Excellent treatise from all points of view.

1768. Rampalle. - "*La Chiromancie naturelle*," by Ronphyle. In-12mo. Paris, Loyson, 1665, aut. ed. Paris, Ribou, 1655.

1769. "*La Science curieuse ou Traité de la Chiromancie*," collected from more serious authors who have treated on this matter... enriched by a great number of figures for the ease of the reader. The whole method of being able to use it. In-4to, numb. pl. on copper giving 1,100 fig. of hands. Paris. F. Clousier, 1667. This work has had several editions.

1771. Tabule. - "*Chiromanciae*," lineis montibus et tuberculis manus constitutionem hominum et fortunae vires ostendentes. In-fol. France, large, 1613.

1772. Tricasse. - "*La Chiromancie*" by Patrice Tricasse de Ceresars, Mantouan, in-8vo, figures of the signs of the hand. Paris, Claude Frémy, 1561. (Bibliogr. by E. Bose.)

1717. Adrian Siclair, spagyric physician born at Puy-en-Velay. - "*Chiromancie royale et nouvelle*" enriched by figures of Moralitez and some Observations on the Qabalah, with some prognoses. Very useful work, in particular for women. Small, in-12mo. Lyon, Daniel Gay, sold by the author at Puits-de-Sel. 1667. (Bibliogr. by Mr. E. Bose.)

Taisnieri. - "*Opus chiromantiae absolutissimae theoriam*" et cutem continens. Cologne, 1562. Contains 190 figures of hands.

Tricasse de Cerosars, 1583. - "*Chiromancie*." Celebrated work; for the most part made with the information of the tradition.

Appendix I

APPENDIX I
The Indiscretions of Writing

This is not a treatise nor even an essay on graphology, it is a process as direct as it is rapid to judge the impulses of the hand according to the forms given to the principal letters. It is the logical conclusion of the whole study of chiromancy and the preface of every truly synthetic treatise on graphomancy. Let us look, then, at how the hand of an ambitious person is going to sign his haughty writing, how that of one modest or violent is going to be revealed to the eye of our readers, especially the female ones, by a simple and nearly instantaneous process.

1. SOCIAL CONDUCT OR THE LETTER M

The capital M is composed generally of three down-strokes, in the current writing. The prideful hand is going to be characterized by the predominance of the first down-stroke (the person who writes) over the second (the person to whom one writes) and over the third (the person of whom one speaks).

In fact, the first down-stroke represents the Me. the second the intimate friends, and the third the indifferent and the masses.

Thus the modest (how rare they are!) make their M where the first down-stroke, which represents them, is *smaller* than the other two, whereas the men accustomed to struggling squash their friends (the second part of the M) between their ambition and the indifferent ones.

2. THE STRUGGLE AGAINST FATALITY OR THE LETTER T

The letter *t* is composed of a vertical bar, which

represents fatality and the exterior conditions of life, and a horizontal bar, which indicates the action of the will of the person who writes on this fatality. From this rule one will easily deduce the consequences.

Thus, the optimists will cross their *t* by going from the earth to the heavens. The pessimists, on the contrary, will cross from heaven to earth. As the bar of the first says: raise the hearts, so does that of the second say: grief and despair come from the false use of the will.

Practical men are going to cross their *t* by skimming the earth: that is to say the lower part of the letter, that which touches the line. One the contrary, pure idealists and the mystics cross their t at the top of the letter in the midst of heaven. Their will is indeed disseminated in projects and theories instead of crawling towards the terrestrial realities as among the pagans and the stewards of the first category.

The beings weak and more nervous than dominating, forget that they have a will and we do not find among them any cross on the *t* or only some at long intervals from each other.

This letter also allows us to see at what moment the will is more energetic. Those whose bars begin thick to end by a progressive thinness have the will only at the start of their undertakings and they quickly fatigue. By contrast, those whose bars begin fine to end in a club, that is to say progressively thickening, are in the same proportion more obstinate as the obstacles are multiplied.

The cholerics and the stubborn envelop the fatality of a shield and bring it in tow of their adventurous life. It is the audacious and the daring that chance favors often, and which constitutes certain personalities of the class so widespread today of "Careerists."

3. DISCRETION OR THE LETTER O OR A

The letter *o* is the symbolic representation of the mouth, so pay close attention to its revelations. If this letter is completely closed then you close your mouth; even in front of your closest friends, you are truly discrete. By contrast, if the top of your lower case *o* and *a* is open, you have an unfortunate tendency to confide under the seal of secrecy many of your intimate affairs to the ones and the others, especially when you are enticed by the confidences of partners. When experience or diplomacy will have rendered you discrete, then your mouth will reflect its mutism in the closing of the *o* and *a*.

4. ORDER IN THE ROOM OR THE LETTER I

The letter *i* is composed of a point surmounting a vertical bar. This point is the representation of the objects, and the bar the representation of the furniture upon which the objects are to be arranged.

Do you put your points exactly above the letter *i*? Then all your papers are carefully arranged on your desk and all is in its place in your room.

By contrast, if the point precedes or follows the letter without happening to be placed directly above, then your desk is encumbered with papers among which you alone are capable of recognizing, and you put order into your affairs only in fits and starts and by periods.

You have order in fits and starts.

But if one seeks in vain the unfortunate point which ought to crown your letter *i*, then you will be the possessor of a room in indescribable disorder where precious papers will be upon the dressing table while the combs will wander upon the desk!

5. HOW ONE DRESSES OR THE LETTER D

The letter *d* is composed of two principal parts: the base and the vertical bar. The round or elliptical base, open or closed, has the same significations as the *o* or *a* (discretion or indiscretion) and represents the individual himself. The vertical bar represents, on the contrary, the exterior door, the mundane attitude and, consequently, the attire.

Here is the general series indicated by the different forms of the loop of the *d*.

The official man, always properly dressed, manifests by an entirely vertical bar without loop; this is the classic *d*.

The one employed in commerce, adorned with a necktie supposed irresistible, turns his loop into a spiral; this is in as bad taste as his attitude.

The artist, who worries nothing about his appearance, makes a very simple flourish, without any pretention.

Finally, the man with eccentric costumes, with gaudy materials and jackets with bizarre cuts, simply reverses his bar of the *d*. He draws it like he dresses: as a caricature.

6. FINAL CONSIDERATIONS ON GRAPHOLOGY

The system of graphology that we have presented is very general and, consequently, does not give any of the numerous details that we find in the special works. Let us add, however, some considerations in this regard.

Sincerity is seen in words enlarging and falsehood in words diminishing and becoming thinner at the end.

The egotists make flourishes with lower concavity, thus bringing back towards the beginning of the mount the stroke they drew at the end.

Appendix I

The avaricious economize the paper as much as their sous. An avaricious letter will be recognized at first glance. There is no margin, the letter begins at the very top of the page to finish at the very bottom, and the writing is as shortened as possible. On the contrary, the squanderers waste their paper and end up putting only four or six lines per page, with enormous white spaces and margins.

Meticulous people and those loving clarity end all their phrases with a small stroke and make many paragraphs.

The poets separate all their letters or, at least, all their syllables; the scholars and reasoners unite in one whole, not only their syllables, but even their words. This division of graphology into intuitive and deductive is the very foundation of the method and recalls exactly the division of the fingers into smooth and gnarled, given by captain d'Arpentigny in the same sense.

PAPUS

APPENDIX II
Philosophy of the Hand

Among all the mysterious initiators that the human soul illumines by its intimate recognitions, the hands are the revealers of our inner kingdoms. They surpass, in eloquent persuasion, all the radiant spaces where linger still, as living expressions, the immaterial rays of our personality.

Sweet effusions of the eyes, abandon of the movements, confidence of the voice, promise of the smile, the hands, animated images of destiny, exceed in fatidic warnings all the insinuations familiar to our ordinary propagators of joy or sorrow. Fatality deposits into our hands, at birth, the secret of its enigmatic designs. And faithful to their roles as premonitory intercessors, they reveal us infallibly by expressive and changing physiognomies, the successive phases of our destiny.

Faces from the past, present, and future appear at once, for the attentive gaze which bends thereto, like a narrow pass, distance and harmonious, whose profiles could have been designed by a supreme Master, according to the laws ordained and necessary, from all eternity.

Thus, the hands retain in their cool palms, suggestive arabesques which resolve, to the initiated minds, the personal enigma of each individuality. However, the lines, fragile webs, prestigious and troubling as a decisive decree of destiny, do not fulfill, alone, their office of warner. The eurhythmy of the fingers, the proportion of the phalanxes, the color of the hand lavish us more their revelatory succors. For, all, in this synthetic part of our being, is a permanent symbol of which the least physiognomies are varied slightly upon our inner tremblings.

There are the hands emaciated and pale, whose elongated fingers have a resemblance to the delicate stems of flowers. The physical fragility and the loss of the nervous forces constitutes, for their frail health, an incessant danger. Their refined sensibility is excessive. They announce the manner of the observation and analysis. Their inner uneasiness never leaves them at rest. And their tormented character is at once hesitant and obstinate. They also denote tendencies towards exclusivism and sentimental egotism.

There are also the thick and short hands which announce physical strength and an accentuated resistance relative to pain. They reveal violence, imprudence, and spontaneity; the taste for risk, dangers, and brutal death, and luck in the efforts.

There are too the pure hands, in the wise and fortunate proportions which betray a perfect equilibrium of the organism as well as intellectual and moral faculties.

The spots of the hand possess, further a great importance. Their signification is modified with their familiar colors. They announce according to the vivacity of the coloring, lasting or passing vicissitudes. We may interpret their presence thus:

Dark spots: painful sorrow to come.

Clear brown spots: passing sorrows.

Red spots: threat of accidents.

The hands of the dying are strewn with dark spots. Moreover, the general hue offers precious indications:

Clear color: uniformity of present and lasting happiness.

Rose color: sound and vigorous health.

Red color: sanguine Temperament, positive, energetic character, refined taste for physical pleasure, little tendency towards the ideal.

Pale color: ill health, uneasy impressionability, somber character, disenchanted.

Thus, the hands possess a language which vibrates in unison with our inner songs. Attentive to our states of soul, they bear, to all always, engraved in their eloquent and sensible palm, the gloom of our sadness's and the mirth of our joys. Intimate mirrors of our thoughts and dreams, the hands faithful to their role of zealous and conscientious scribe, inscribes by a greyish or rose- colored point, upon the register of their flesh, the melancholic emotion of the vigil of the enchanted promise of the next day.

Fraya
(Paris, October, 1917)

Appendix III

APPENDIX III
PAPUS, according to Graphology, Chiromancy, and Physiognomy

∗∗∗

[handwritten letter in French, signed Papus]

Translation: True esotericism is the Science of the cardiac adaptations.

The Sentiment is sole creator in all the planes, the idea is creator only in the human mental plane, it reaches only with difficulty the superior Nature. Prayer is the great mystery and may, for the one who perceives the influence of Christ, God come in the flesh, permit one to receive the highest influences in action on the Divine Plane.

PAPUS.

A. Graphology ("PHANEG")

If graphology can inform incontestably on the inner movements of the Spirit, according to the forms of one's graphism, it is incapable, beyond a certain degree, of making anything known on the very nature of the Spirit; and nothing in the writing of a Master will make a presentiment of his spiritual elevation. The writing of Papus will show us the man that all can see; we will find here his aptitudes, his intelligence, his qualities of heart, but nothing more. It will, however, be interesting, especially for those who know the doctor Encausse through his books but have never seen him. Let us remind ourselves, then, that it is the *exterior* man alone that we are going to rapidly study.

The writing of Papus is small, rounded, harmonious, in general not very stressed, slightly rising, consistent, and contains many curves. It indicates at once benevolence, gentleness, calm activity, equilibrated intelligence.

The letters are sometimes tied together, sometimes separated. There would be rather an excess, a slight excess of intuition, but this one is always reasoned intuitively, one could say, if the two terms did not clash.

The *sensibility* is very keen, but it is so dominated, and reasoned too, that it appears very little in the graphism whose look is straight rather than inclined; yet certain words reveal it with an attentive study.

The *will* is real, but exercises itself above all in the manner of domination, of commandment. One senses that a writing where this sign is repeated so often ought to belong to the head of a movement, to a man called to command everywhere. The will is consistent, but yet manifests itself rarely under the form of stubbornness.

In the intellectual plane, Papus does not hold on to his ideas when he has recognized them as false, and his mental state is in constant evolution: "Always better, ever higher," such could be his motto.

If we find neither stubbornness nor resolution, the

Appendix III

signs of a sometimes obstinate perseverance are very clear and undeniable.

The bars of the T's rounded into a semi-circle are encountered rather frequently. I have found that this sign symbolizes quite exactly the very progress of the will: not very strong at the beginning of an affair, it increases progressively with the difficulties, then decreases if the goal is not reached. This is only sometimes.

If we now examine the graphism of Papus from the point of view of the sentiments of goodness, gentleness, gratitude, and benevolence, we find therein all the classical signs with a consistency and a frequency which shows us to what degree these qualities are developed in him.

Consequently, we do not see any of the signs of disdain, annoyance, bitterness, or raillery; at the very most the taste for humor, sometimes sharp, never ill-natured, could be recognized in certain bars of the T.

The firmness of the graphism shows us the combative, the active par excellence; the not very compressed letters let us see a generous heart, always ready to give of his time, his ideas, or his money.

The small hooks of Egotism are nearly completely missing in the writing of Papus; the grave accents often extending over the whole word shows us the radiant, the devoted such as he really is.

Let us pass on to the *intelligence*. It is by nature, by Temperament, very clearly analytical, without trifle, rapidly seeing all the details and forming for itself a clear idea of things; but moreover it is become synthetic by the will and work. It unites, therefore, these two faculties, and from their union comes the aptitudes for popularization, the classifying clearness, the faculties of adaptation.

The *tastes* of Papus are artistic but not very cultivated, his aptitudes are varied. We note especially in the graphism the clearness, precision, logic, and aptitude for the sciences.

The flourish also indicates a great commercial competency, and diplomacy is certified by the writing often not very readable.

The initials, small in general, indicate true Humility, Simplicity. A curious thing: the E of Encausse is nearly always smaller than the P of Papus. It attests that Papus gives much more importance to his role as head of Occidental Occultism in France, than to his true personality.

The writing also reveals to us calm without nervousness, nor exaltation (the enthusiasm which actually exists with Papus is too deep, too inner to appear in the graphism, this is in favor of what I said in the beginning), real sincerity, an open heart. But the over-inked letters, often twice closed, indicate at the same time a being excessively closed and discrete when it is necessary. There is no guile here, but finesse and competency.

B. Chiromancy (Mme. "FRAYA")

A general impression of strength and power becomes clear from the hand of Papus. The signs are numerous of a true and active goodness, ceaselessly seeking to be realized in life. The feeble will in reality is replaced by activity, the strength of inertia, obstinacy. Often, the fear of doing harm and not obeying his duty renders Papus indecisive; but he always ends up achieving his ends. A combatted timidity causes sudden blows of audacity and which may completely deceive superficial observers on his account.

The harmony between the palm and the fingers indicates equilibrium, great tendencies towards optimism, from where originate in part, the strength, radiance, and

Appendix III

comfort that he spreads around him.

The short fingers indicate the lack of positive sense, profound and synthetic intelligence which sees the details with difficulty.

We also find the love of all that is simple; an astonishing classifying memory, the science of forgetting bad things, an extraordinary medical intuition, real artistic tastes, though not having been cultivated.

Papus is above all a realizer. His very thoughts immediately take, so to speak, an objective form, tending to never remain in the plane of reverie.

He cannot see disagreeable things, he detests debates and prefers to yield and to allow himself to be directed in certain cases rather than defend himself. He uses his energy beyond the customary circle of his life.

The character of Papus is full of contradiction and renders him very difficult to understand; the motive of his actions most often escape the observer. He is confident, but life has rendered him cautious. He is gentle because he fears his violent impulses. He is given to enthusiasm, and yet is capable of profound discretion. He is not practical, but yet he possesses perfectly all that may simplify life and render it more comfortable.

He adores the simple life and leads the most complicated existence there is. He is a mystic, but his mysticism comes not from the love of the marvelous. He proceeds from observation and has a clear and explicable basis. He has the spirit of a jokester and is very sentimental, capable of lasting and sincere passions. He is never more serious than when he jests; and, all while solving the greatest problems of philosophy, he may amuse himself like a child. In conclusion, we say that in his hand, numerous stars indicate his work of popularization, his mission, and his popularity. His health is robust, but subject to violent attacks which he patiently endures.

C. Physiognomy ("PHANEG")

Types: Moon dominating, Jupiter, then Mars (a little).

Rounded forehead, disengaged from the top and thickset, (the Moon) giving an active, strong, fruitful, intuitive imagination; an abundance of strong, varied, intellectual sensations; a lively, assimilating intelligence; at times, dullness in ideas (massive form of the forehead). Religiosity.

The rounded, silky (Moon), curved (Jupiter) brows give: intellectual activity, ease of work, good nervous organization of the brain, a little susceptibility and pride very combatted. The wounds of vanity will be sustained in silence and with courage. The hidden eyes, the fine, direct, observing gaze (Moon) signifies: ability to turn situations to his advantage. Analysis by impression rather than by reflection. Sense of the diagnostic. They reveal an intimate vision of things, ordinarily clear.

The short, rounded nose (Moon and Jupiter) gives: intuition, finesse, competency, business sense. Benevolence, great gentleness.

The plump, rounded cheeks (Jupiter): much goodness. Sense of protection. Fidelity in friendships. Affability.

The rounded mouth (Moon), advancing a little (Saturn) signifies: intimate sadness, concentration of thought; one keeps deeply to oneself the essence of certain tendencies and certain sentiments. Reserved.

The short and strong chin (Mars), the short and squat face (Mars) gives activity, energy, the sense of commandment. They also give a taste for expenses in different things.

In short, the Moon dominates strongly and brings the spirit upon the superior planes, it gives intellectuality, a very gentle nature, very intuitive, prone to the study of the superior sciences. The Moon brings danger through water, but here the waters to fear are superior, it is Astral.

The Moon is good, but Jupiter is unfortunate. Nevertheless, it always brings its qualities: goodness, affability, obligingness, gentleness, and benevolence.

To the evil influences is opposed the able, good-natured man. By contrast, he is serious and there arises from his person a character upon which friends may count.

Mars, which manifests itself by the squat form, is favorable; it brings a fighting character, strong energy which allows one to repair the losses and to struggle against the envious and malevolent hostilities; it supports the lunarian influence, soft by nature. By contrast, it brings its faults, that is to say the excess of diffusion, which is harmful to the success of any undertaking. Mars also brings the spirit of authority and domination.

Saturn, whose influence is extremely weak, gives logic, the spirit of classification, and prudence. There are moments of bitterness and disabused instances which come from its influence. In short, this physiognomy is intuitive, profound, energetic, calm relaxed, ordered. We see here the strength of work (squat form); the comprehension of the superior planes (disengaged forehead); benevolence and goodness are so many energies which emanate from the subject and promise him finally an honorific recompense.

There is threat of accident to the leg or at the very least weakness of this side. The moon gives longevity, but *Jupiter* shortens the existence, and necessitates attentions from the age of 55.

ENDNOTES

1. This passage is extracted from the *Traité méthodique de Science Occulte*.
2. *Encyclopédie du XIXe siècle*, supplementary art. *Theosophie*.
3. See Malfati de Monteregio: *La Mathèse*.
4. See in the continuation of this chapter the details of this subject.
5. See figure 36.
6. See figure 38.
7. See figure 39.
8. Vigot, publisher, Paris (out of print).
9. Each line is connected to the designations given with respect to Saturn and that we have judged useless to repeat.
10. The hemiplegia which paralyzes the right side of man or the left side of man while leaving one of the two intact proves this division. Each hand corresponds to the inverse brain, the right hand to the left hemisphere and vice-versa.
11. In a work published in the "*Revue Scientifique*" it relates that the lines of the thumb allow the establishment of a sign of recognition of each individual and form groupings that may be classified.

www.ingramcontent.com/pod-product-compliance
Lightning Source LLC
Chambersburg PA
CBHW051841090426
42736CB00011B/1907